WITHDRAWN

the very best of

Contemporary Christian

words and music

a collection of over
375 songs
for Piano, Vocal, Guitar,
Organ and
all ``C'' instruments

*Special thanks to Randy Cox for
his valuable assistance.*

ISBN 0-88188-489-8

A *J. Aaron Brown & Associates* Publication
in association with

HAL LEONARD
PUBLISHING
CORPORATION

Home Office: National Sales Office:
960 East Mark Street   8112 West Bluemound Road
Winona MN 55987   Milwaukee WI 53213

the very best of
Contemporary Christian
words and music

This unique compilation of Contemporary Christian songs, written and recorded by America's favorite songwriters and recording artists of Christian music, offers three convenient listings of the songs that appear in this book:

■ In the ALPHABETICAL LISTING, the song titles are listed alphabetically, followed by the name of the recording artist. The page on which each song can be found is the number to the left of the song title.

■ In the RECORDING ARTIST LISTING on page 6, the artists names are listed alphabetically followed by the songs each has recorded.

■ In the COMPOSER/LYRICIST INDEX on page 11, all music composer and lyricist names are listed individually in alphabetical sequence, followed by their respective songs.

ALPHABETICAL LISTING

3

E

81 EAGLE SONG — *The Imperials*
83 EASTER SONG — *2nd Chapter Of Acts; Keith Green*
86 EL SHADDAI — *Amy Grant*
86 ELIJAH — *Richard Mullins*
88 EMMANUEL — *Amy Grant*
84 END OF THE BOOK — *Michael W. Smith*
90 EVENING SONG — *The Harper Twins*
85 EVERY STEP OF THE WAY — *Kathy Troccoli,
          Billy Sqrague*
88 EVERYWHERE I GO — *Amy Grant*
90 EXODUS SONG, THE

F

91 FAIREST OF TEN THOUSAND —
          Tanya Goodman; Lulu Roman Smith
92 FAITH TAKES A VISION — *James Ward*
93 FAITH WALKIN' PEOPLE — *Amy Grant*
94 FAN MAIL — *Tanya Goodman*
96 FATHER'S EYES — *Amy Grant*
95 FINALLY — *Gary Chapman*
97 FIND A HURT AND HEAL IT — *Debby Boone*
98 FIND A WAY — *Amy Grant*
100 FIRST STONE, THE — *Joe English*
102 FLAWLESS — *Kim Noblitt*
103 FOLLOWING THE KING — *White Heart*
104 FOLLOWING YOU — *The Harper Twins*
99 FOR THE LOVE OF IT
105 FOR UNTO US — *Larnelle Harris*
100 FOREVER — *Cynthia Clawson*
106 FORGIVEN — *David Meece*
110 FORGIVING EYES — *Michael Card*
107 FRIENDLY FIRE — *Dennis Agajanian*
108 FRIENDS — *Michael W. Smith*
109 FROM THIS MOMENT — *The Harper Twins*

G

114 GENTLE HANDS — *Truth*
112 GIVE THEM ALL TO JESUS — *Evie*
112 GOD'S OWN FOOL — *Michael Card*
111 GOD'S WONDERFUL PEOPLE — *The Gaither Trio*
116 GOLIATH — *Scott Wesley Brown*
115 GOT TO LET IT GO — *Amy Grant*
120 GOT TO TELL SOMEBODY — *Don Francisco*
122 GOTTA HAVE THE REAL THING — *Rick Riso*
118 GRAVE ROBBER — *Petra*
117 GREAT IS THE LORD — *Michael W. Smith*
119 GREATER IS HE THAT IS IN ME — *The Downings*

H

124 HE HOLDS THE KEYS — *Steve Green*
126 HE ROLLED AWAY THE STONE — *Michele Pillar*
123 HE SET MY LIFE TO MUSIC — *Barbara Mandrell*
121 HE WAS THERE ALL THE TIME
127 HE WILL CARRY YOU — *Scott Wesley Brown*
128 HE'LL SHINE HIS LIGHT ON YOU — *Michele Pillar*
130 HE'S ALIVE — *Don Francisco*
132 HE'S ONLY A PRAYER AWAY — *Shirley Caesar;
          Ben Moore*
134 HEART OF THE SEEKER, THE — *Tanya Goodman*
131 HEAVEN FELL LIKE RAIN (WHEN HE SPOKE) —
          Keith Longbotham
135 HEAVENLY FATHER — *Billy Sprague*
129 HEIRLOOMS — *Amy Grant*
134 HELP ME LOVE MY BROTHER — *Tanya Goodman*
136 HERE HE COMES WITH MY HEART —
          Leslie Phillips
137 HERE I AM — *Russ Taff*
138 HIS GRACE IS GREATER — *Larnelle Harris*

133 HOLD ON — *Micki Fuhrman; The Cruse Family*
132 HOLINESS — *Don Francisco*
140 HOLLOW EYES — *Petra*
141 HOLY GROUND — *Davis/Pedigo*
138 HOLY, HOLY — *Kathy Troccoli*
142 HOLY IS HIS NAME — *John Michael Talbot*
144 HOME WHERE I BELONG — *B.J. Thomas*
142 HOSANNA — *Michael W. Smith*
148 HOSANNA, GLORIA — *Farrell & Farrell*
144 HOW CAN THEY LIVE WITHOUT JESUS? —
          Keith Green
146 HOW COULD I EVER SAY NO —
          Jamie Owens-Collins
150 HOW EXCELLENT IS THY NAME — *Larnelle Harris*
146 HOW MAJESTIC IS YOUR NAME — *Sandi Patti*
147 HYMN — *Randy Stonehill*

I

149 I AM HE — *Terry Talbot*
154 I AM LOVED — *The Gaither Trio*
152 I AM SURE — *Michael W. Smith*
150 I BELONG TO YOU — *Kathy Troccoli*
153 I CAN SEE — *David Meece*
156 I DEDICATE ALL MY LOVE TO YOU — *Teri DeSario*
162 I HAVE DECIDED — *Amy Grant*
160 I JUST FEEL LIKE SOMETHING GOOD IS
          ABOUT TO HAPPEN — *The Gaither Trio*
164 I KNOW — *Michael W. Smith*
166 I LOVE A LONELY DAY — *Amy Grant*
154 I LOVE YOU — *Amy Grant*
166 I WALKED TODAY — *Scott Wesley Brown*
159 I WANT TO BE A CLONE — *Steve Taylor*
158 I WANT TO KNOW CHRIST — *Larnelle Harris*
156 I WANT TO MAKE A DIFFERENCE — *Michele Pillar*
168 I'D RATHER BELIEVE IN YOU — *The Imperials*
160 I'M GONNA FLY — *Amy Grant*
174 I'M UP — *Michael W. Smith*
169 I'VE HEARD THE THUNDER — *Leon Patillo*
170 I'VE JUST SEEN JESUS — *Larnelle Harris & Sandi Patti*
167 IF ONLY — *Kathy Troccoli*
172 IN A LITTLE WHILE — *Amy Grant*
162 IN HIS NAME — *White Heart*
174 IN THE NAME OF THE LORD — *Sandi Patti*
173 IN THE PROMISED LAND — *The Imperials*
178 IT IS GOOD — *Celeste Clydesdale*
176 IT WAS ENOUGH — *Gary McSpadden*
180 IT'S JUST THE FIRST FAREWELL — *Tony Elenburg*
177 IT'S NOT A SONG — *Amy Grant*

J

181 JEHOVAH — *Amy Grant*
182 JERICHO — *The Imperials*
183 JESUS CALL YOUR LAMBS — *Sheilah Walsh &
          Cliff Richmond*
184 JESUS IN YOUR HEART — *Connie Scott*
178 JESUS IS LORD — *Continental Singers*
185 JESUS, LORD TO ME — *Gary McSpadden*
186 JESUS NEVER FAILS — *Truth*
188 JUDE DOXOLOGY — *Billy Sprague*

K

189 KEEP THE FLAME BURNING — *Debby Boone;
          Phil Driscoll*
186 KEEPIN' MY EYES ON YOU — *Twila Paris*
190 KING OF WHO I AM, THE — *Lulu Roman Smith &
          Russ Taff; Tanya Goodman*
190 KINGDOM OF LOVE — *Scott Wesley Brown*
192 KNOWN BY THE SCARS — *Michael Card*

RECORDING ARTISTS LISTING

D

Davis/Pedigo
141 Holy Ground

DeGarmo & Key
27 Alleluia, Christ Is Coming
72 Destined To Win
193 Let The Whole World Sing
306 Six, Six, Six

Teri DeSario
38 Battleline
52 Celebrate
156 I Dedicate All My Love To You
240 No More Night
326 Tapestry

Jessy Dixon
60 Celebrate The Lord
296 Silent Partner

The Downings
119 Greater Is He That Is In Me

Phil Driscoll
189 Keep The Flame Burning
224 Messiah

E

Tony Elenburg
180 It's Just The First Farewell

Joe English
100 The First Stone

Evie
37 Born Again
112 Give Them All To Jesus
254 Oh, How He Loves You And Me
315 Special Delivery

F

Farrell & Farrell
148 Hosanna, Gloria
259 People In A Box

First Call
346 Undivided

John Fischer
213 Lord Of The Dance

Don Francisco
120 Got To Tell Somebody
130 He's Alive
132 Holiness

Steve Fry
362 We Can Change The World

Micki Fuhrman
133 Hold On

G

The Gaither Trio
111 God's Wonderful People
154 I Am Loved
160 I Just Feel Like Something Good Is About To Happen
351 We Are So Blessed

Gaither Vocal Band
45 Blessed Messiah
242 No Other Name But Jesus
241 Not By Might, Not By Power
264 Passin' The Faith Along
330 That's When The Angels Rejoice

Glenn Garrett
367 You Are Jehovah

Glad
221 Maker Of My Heart
231 The More I Know Of You

Rusty Goodman
230 Mizpah

Tanya Goodman
22 Ageless Dancer
70 The Darkness Is Under His Feet
91 Fairest Of Ten Thousand
94 Fan Mail
134 The Heart Of The Seeker
134 Help Me Love My Brother
190 The King Of Who I Am
204 Let Them Go
206 Lift Him Up
207 Love Everybody In The World
209 Love Never Fails
268 Promises
274 Quiet Place
337 Time To Start Building Again
361 We've Got A Secret
382 Worthy
380 You're The Singer

Amy Grant
34 Angels
34 Arms Of Love
49 Brand New Start
79 Don't Run Away
82 Doubly Good To You
86 El Shaddai
88 Emmanuel
88 Everywhere I Go
93 Faith Walkin' People
96 Father's Eyes
98 Find A Way
115 Got To Let It Go
129 Heirlooms
162 I Have Decided
166 I Love A Lonely Day
154 I Love You
160 I'm Gonna Fly
172 In A Little While
177 It's Not A Song
181 Jehovah
200 Love Of Another Kind
229 Mountain Top
244 The Now And The Not Yet
256 Old Man's Rubble
255 On And On (Love Song)
257 Open Arms
272 The Prodigal
278 Raining On The Inside
290 Sharayah
304 Sing Your Praise To The Lord
305 Singing A Love Song
293 So Glad
320 Straight Ahead
327 Thy Word
341 Tomorrow
343 Too Late
378 What A Difference You've Made In My Life
370 Where Do you Hide Your Heart
374 Who To Listen To
372 Wise Up

Keith Green
31 Asleep In The Light
83 Easter Song
144 How Can They Live Without Jesus?
243 Oh Lord You're Beautiful

Steve Green
52 Calvary's Love
54 Celebrate His Good Life
124 He Holds The Keys
194 Lamb Of Glory
211 Love Found A Way
222 Mighty Fortress
268 People Need The Lord
266 Praise To The King
270 Proclaim The Glory Of The Lord
332 That's Where The Joy Comes From

N

The Nelons
22 All Rise

New Song
63 Conversation Peace

Kim Noblitt
61 Champion Of The Battle
102 Flawless
349 Unveil Your Glory

O

Michael & Stormie Omartian
44 Believing For The Best In You

P

Twila Paris
74 Do I Trust You
186 Keepin' My Eyes On You
199 Lamb Of God
281 Runner
358 The Warrior Is A Child

Leon Patillo
59 Cornerstone
169 I've Heard The Thunder
218 Love Calling
251 One Thing Leads To Another
308 The Sky's The Limit
318 Star Of The Morning

Sandi Patti
41 Because Of Who You Are
72 The Day He Wore My Crown
146 How Majestic Is Your Name
170 I've Just Seen Jesus
174 In The Name Of The Lord
198 Let There Be Praise
216 Love In Any Language
236 More Than Wonderful
244 O Magnify The Lord
265 Pour On The Power
287 Shepherd Of My Heart
292 Shine Down
301 Sing To The Lord
314 Somebody Believed
332 There Is A Savior
347 Unshakable Kingdom
350 Upon This Rock
352 Via Dolorosa
353 Was It A Morning Like This
359 We Shall Behold Him
364 We Will See Him As He Is

Dan Peek
28 All Things Are Possible
74 Doer Of The Word

Petra
33 Beat The System
66 The Coloring Song
118 Grave Robber
140 Hollow Eyes
232 More Power To Ya
235 Not Of This World
277 The Road To Zion

Leslie Phillips
42 By My Spirit
136 Here He Comes With
    My Heart
317 Strength Of My Life
384 Your Kindness

Michele Pillar
126 He Rolled Away The Stone
128 He'll Shine His Light On You
156 I Want To Make A Difference
210 Look Who Loves You Now

Ponder, Sykes & Wright
262 Only Child

R

"Race Is On" Musical
342 Trust The Lord

The Rambos
42 Behold The Lamb

Cliff Richmond
183 Jesus Call Your Lambs

Rick Riso
122 Gotta Have The Real Thing

S

Phillip Sandifer
253 On My Way

Connie Scott
184 Jesus In Your Heart
214 Lord Of Glory

2nd Chapter Of Acts
83 Easter Song
224 Mansion Builder
271 Rejoice
325 Takin' The Easy Way

Servant
360 We Are The Light

Trent Sisemore
78 Don't Look Back
280 Right Direction

Lulu Roman Smith
91 Fairest Of Ten Thousand
190 The King Of Who I Am
230 Mizpah
294 Shopping List
383 Your Grace Still Amazes Me

Michael W. Smith
18 A Way
24 All I Needed To Say
84 End Of The Book
108 Friends
117 Great Is The Lord
142 Hosanna
152 I Am Sure
164 I Know
174 I'm Up
276 The Race Is On
340 To The Praise Of His
    Glorious Grace

Sonlight
258 On One Condition

Billy Sprague
85 Every Step Of The Way
135 Heavenly Father
188 Jude Doxology
365 What A Way To Go

Randy Stonehill
147 Hymn

T _____

Russ Taff
40 Be Still My Soul
137 Here I Am
190 The King Of Who I Am
279 Rock Solid
295 Silent Love
354 We Will Stand

John Michael Talbot
142 Holy Is His Name

Terry Talbot
149 I Am He

The Talleys
333 Thinkin' About Home

Steve Taylor
159 I Want To Be A Clone
226 Meltdown (At Madame
    Tussaud's)

B.J. Thomas
48 Born To Fly
144 Home Where I Belong
270 Pray For Me
328 Teach Me To See
375 Without A Doubt

Kelly Nelon Thompson
40 Baruch Hashem Adonai
234 Miracle Man
310 The Singer
382 Worthy
383 Your Grace Still Amazes
    Me

Terry Toler
262 Only Child
333 Thinkin' About Home

Kathy Troccoli
85 Every Step Of The Way
138 Holy, Holy
150 I Belong To You
167 If Only
228 Mighty Lord
319 Stubborn Love

Truth
114 Gentle Hands
186 Jesus Never Fails
238 A New Heart
302 Sing Unto Him
308 Somebody's Prayin'
331 Throw Me The Keys
363 What Can I Do

J.J. Turner
35 Be A Friend
207 Love Everybody In
    The World
262 Only Child
310 The Singer
336 Think Big

W _____

Christy Walker
78 Don't Look Back
280 Right Direction

Sheilah Walsh
183 Jesus Call Your Lambs

James Ward
92 Faith Takes A Vision

Rose Warnke
35 Be A Friend
207 Love Everybody In
    The World

Wayne Watson
47 Born In Zion
212 Lookin' Out For
    Number One
222 Man In The Middle

White Heart
103 Following The King
162 In His Name
274 Quiet Love
354 Vital Signs
356 We Are His Hands

Aaron Wilburn
48 Born To Fly
234 Miracle Man
270 Pray For Me
276 Resident Power
282 Run With The Power

Kelly Willard
248 Nothing But The Blood

Deniece Williams
234 My Soul Desire
312 So Glad I Know

The Winans
344 Tomorrow

Pat Wroten
200 Lambs In The Valley
249 Over The Mountain
378 You Are The Poem

COMPOSER/LYRICIST INDEX

Vickie McCall
254 On The Water

Dony McGuire
350 Upon This Rock
376 Wounded Soldier

Reba McGuire
377 Wounded Soldier

Phill McHugh
18 Above The Storm
20 All Over The World
39 Believers
52 Calvary's Love
138 His Grace Is Greater
174 In The Name Of The Lord
194 Lamb Of Glory
211 Love Found A Way
268 People Need The Lord
284 The Red Sea Parted
369 Where There Is Love

Gary McSpadden
185 Jesus, Lord To Me
242 No Other Name But Jesus

David Meece
30 And You Know It's Right
106 Forgiven
153 I Can See
357 We Are The Reason
379 You Can Go

Jerry Michael
99 For The Love Of It

Lonna Miller
310 The Singer

Jon Mohr
124 He Holds The Key
216 Love In Any Language
264 Passin' The Faith Along

Dennis W. Morgan
123 He Set My Life To Music

Richard Mullins
82 Doubly Good To You
86 Elijah
200 Love Of Another Kind
250 O Come All Ye Faithful
304 Sing Your Praise To The Lord
316 Sparrow Watcher

Kathleen Murdock
99 For The Love Of It

Michael James Murphy
71 The Darker The Night

N _____

Phil Naish
18 Above The Storm
116 Goliath
202 Let The Wind Blow
381 Where Are The Other Nine?

Carol (Connie) Nelson
189 Keep The Flame Burning

Greg Nelson
20 All Over The World
52 Calvary's Love
54 Celebrate His Good Life
138 His Grace Is Greater
166 I Walked Today
185 Jesus, Lord To Me
194 Lamb Of Glory
211 Love Found A Way
268 People Need The Lord
284 The Red Sea Parted
285 Somebody's Brother
332 There Is A Savior
351 We Are So Blessed
382 When Answers Aren't Enough
369 Where There Is Love

Hal Newman
35 Be A Friend
132 He's Only A Prayer Away
318 Spreadin' Like Wildfire

Rachel Newman
35 Be A Friend
318 Spreadin' Like Wildfire

O _____

Spooner Oldham
132 He's Only A Prayer Away

Jerome Olds
338 Trains Up In The Sky

Michael Omartian
26 All My Life
44 Believing For The Best In You
168 I'd Rather Believe
262 One More Song For You
328 The Time Is Now
345 The Trumpet Of Jesus

Stormie Omartian
26 All My Life
44 Believing For The Best In You
168 I'd Rather Believe
262 One More Song For You
263 Praise The Lord, He Never
      Changes
328 The Time Is Now
345 The Trumpet Of Jesus

Paul Overstreet
133 Hold On

Carol Owens
358 The Warrior

Jimmy Owens
358 The Warrior

Jamie Owens-Collins
146 How Could I Ever Say No
203 Look How Far You've Come

P _____

John Parenti
368 When God Ran

Starla Paris
281 Runner

Twila Paris
186 Keepin' My Eyes On You
199 Lamb Of God
281 Runner
358 The Warrior Is A Child

David Parks
135 Heavenly Father

Leon Patillo
59 Cornerstone
169 I've Heard The Thunder
218 Love Calling
251 One Thing Leads To Another
308 The Sky's The Limit
318 Star Of The Morning

Gary S. Paxton
121 He Was There All The Time
242 No Shortage

Dan Peek
28 All Things Are Possible

Justin Peters
39 Believers
100 The First Stone

Leslie Phillips
42 By My Spirit
136 Here He Comes With My Heart
317 Strength Of My Life
384 Your Kindness

Michele Pillar
128 He'll Shine His Light On You
156 I Want To Make A Difference

T _____

Russ Taff
40 Be Still My Soul
81 Eagle Song
137 Here I Am
295 Silent Love
354 We Will Stand

Tori Taff
40 Be Still My Soul
81 Eagle Song
137 Here I Am
295 Silent Love
354 We Will Stand

John Michael Talbot
142 Holy Is His Name

Terry Talbot
149 I Am He

Bobby Taylor
22 Ageless Dancer

Steve Taylor
159 I Want To Be A Clone
226 Meltdown (At Madame Tussaud's)

Steven V. Taylor
36 The Battle Is The Lord's

Pat Terry
144 Home Where I Belong

B.J. Thomas
270 Pray For Me
375 Without A Doubt

Gloria Thomas
270 Pray For Me
328 Teach Me To See

Keith Thomas
219 Make My Heart Your Home
260 One Last Goodbye
275 Right Where You Are

John W. Thompson
70 Count Me In
69 Count The Cost
86 El Shaddai

Becky Thurman
100 The First Stone
102 Flawless

Geoff Thurman
100 The First Stone
102 Flawless
117 Great Is The Lord
266 Praise To The King

Terry Toler
78 Don't Look Back
236 New Day
262 Only Child
333 Thinkin' About Home

Sloan Towner
319 Stubborn Love

Kathy Troccoli
167 If Only
278 Raining On The Inside

Dick Tunney
105 For Unto Us
150 How Excellent Is Thy Name
198 Let There Be Praise
244 O Magnify The Lord
287 Shepherd Of My Heart
363 What Can I Do

Melodie Tunney
105 For Unto Us
150 How Excellent Is Thy Name
198 Let There Be Praise
244 O Magnify The Lord
258 On One Condition
313 Sound His Praise
346 Undivided

J.J. Turner
336 Think Big

V _____

Beverly Vowell
380 You're The Singer

W _____

Tricia Walker
40 Baruch Hashem Adonai
300 Sing The Glory Of His Name

J.L. Wallace
126 He Rolled Away The Stone

Byron Walls
230 Mizpah

James Ward
92 Faith Takes A Vision
150 I Belong To You

Wayne Watson
212 Lookin' Out For Number One

Jim Weber
51 Can You Reach My Friend
85 Every Step Of The Way
102 Flawless
134 The Heart Of The Seeker
178 It Is Good
305 Singing A Love Song
342 Trust The Lord

Charles Wesley
62 Christ The Lord Is Risen Today

Charles Aaron Wilburn
48 Born To Fly
63 Conversation Peace
234 Miracle Man
270 Pray For Me
276 Resident Power
282 Run With The Power
328 Teach Me To See
372 Who Is He
380 You're The Singer

Deniece Williams
312 So Glad I Know

Shirley Caesar Williams
54 Celebration
372 Who Is He

Carvin Winans
344 Tomorrow

Debra Winans
344 Tomorrow

Lanny Wolfe
111 God's Wonderful People
236 More Than Wonderful

Mark Wright
374 Who To Listen To

A WAY

By MICHAEL W. SMIT
GARY CHAPMAN & TIM MARS

ABOVE THE STORM

By Phill McHugh & Phil Nais

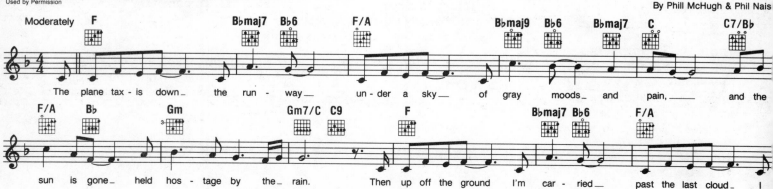

ADONAI

By DAVID C. MART...

Ad - o - nai, cre - ate in me___ a clean___ heart,___
my con - trite heart___ I___ sac - ri - fice,

Ad - o - nai.___ Ad - o - nai, re - new the right
Ad - o - nai.___ Ad - o - nai, *(Instrumental)*

___ spir - it___ in___ me, Ad - o - nai,

Cast me not___ from Your___ pres - ence.___ Re - store the joy___ of my

___ sal - va - tion, A - do - nai.___ Ad - o - nai.
Oh,___ A - do - nai,___ Ad - o - nai, the song I sing

___ shall___ be Thy praise,___ Ad - o - nai.___ Ad - o -

Repeat and Fa...

nai. *(vocal and instrumental ad lib.)*

ALL OVER THE WORLD

By PHILL McHUGH & GREG NELSON

With movement

CHORUS

All O - ver The World___ All O - ver The World___ God's Spir - it is

mov - ing___ All O - ver The World___ All O - ver The World

AGELESS DANCER

Words and Music by
JESS LEARY & BOBBY TAYLOR

ALL RISE

By BABBI MASON

All I Needed To Say

By MICHAEL W. SMITH,
GARY CHAPMAN & AMY GRANT

ARMY OF THE LORD

Words and Music by BRENT LAMB

ALL MY LIFE

By STORMIE & MICHAEL OMARTIAN

ALLELUIA, CHRIST IS COMING

By ED DeGARMO & DANA KEY

ALL THINGS ARE POSSIBLE

By CHRIS CHRISTIAN & DAN PEE

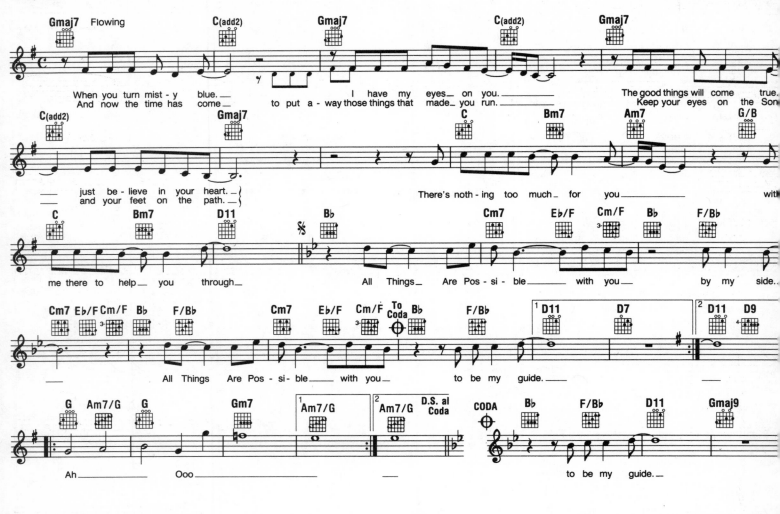

When you turn mist-y blue.___ I have my eyes___ on you.___ The good things will come true.___
And now the time has come to put a-way those things that made__ you run. Keep your eyes on the Son

___ just be-lieve in your heart.___ { There's noth-ing too much__ for you_____ with
___ and your feet on the path.___ }

me there to help__ you through___ All Things__ Are Pos-si-ble_____ with you___ by my side.

All Things Are Pos-si-ble___ with you___ to be my guide._____

Ah___ Ooo_____ ___ to be my guide._____

ARISE, SHINE

By WENDELL BURTON & MARTY GOET

Joyfully, in 4

A peo-ple in dark-ness,___ they stum-ble with eyes___ that can-not see,___
Be-hold the new Zi-on,___ set__ up so high on His ho-ly hill,___

___ a-lone___ in the night, they hope__ for the light, and long for the bright-ness.___
___ a torch__ in the night, a ci-ty of light, a-blaze with His bright-ness.___

But on___ the ho-ri-zon, He comes__ with a glo-ry of__ the sun,
Oh see__ your Re-deem-er, hear His voice__ like the roar of a thou-sand seas,

like the rush__ of a stream, to heal and re-deem, His ra-di-ant gleam -ing.___
a-wake__ you who sleep, though the climb may be steep, He calls to His peo-ple.

AND YOU KNOW IT'S RIGHT

By MICHAEL W. SMITH
BROWN BANNISTER & DAVID MEECE

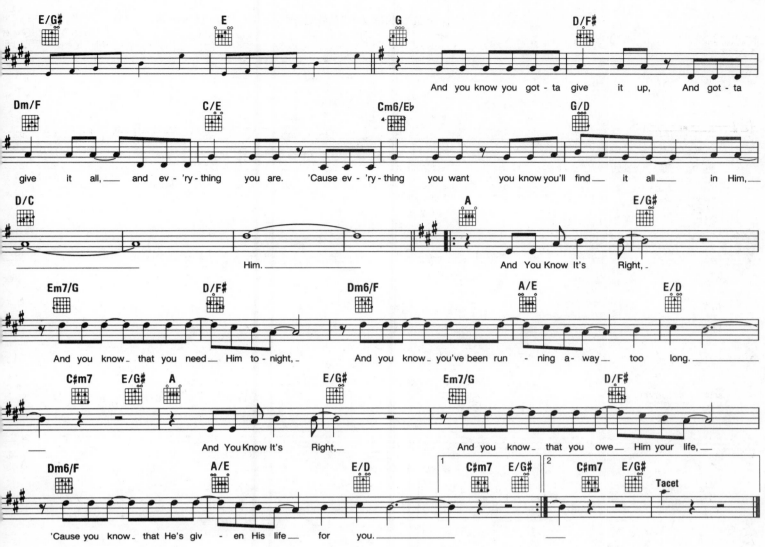

ASLEEP IN THE LIGHT

'78 Birdwing Music/Cherry Lane Music Publishing Co., Inc./Ears to Hear Music

By KEITH GREEN

With feeling

"Oh, bless me, Lord, do you see all the peo-ple sink-ing down. Don't you
O-pen up, bless me, Lord," you know it's all I ev-er hear. No one
O-pen up and give your-self a-way. You see the

care, don't you care, are you gon-na let them drown. How can you be so numb not to
aches, no one hurts, no one e-ven shed one tear. But He cries, He weeps, He bleeds, and He
need, you hear the cries, so how can you de-lay? God's call-ing you're the one, but like

care if they come? You close your eyes and pre-tend the job's done.
cares for your needs, And you just lay back and keep soak-ing it
Jo-nah you run, He's told you to speak but you keep hold-ing it

BEAT THE SYSTEM

Words and Music by
BOB HARTMAN

ARMS OF LOVE

By MICHAEL W. SMITH
GARY CHAPMAN & AMY GRANT

ANGELS

By MICHAEL W. SMITH, GARY CHAPMAN
BROWN BANNISTER & AMY GRANT

BE A FRIEND

Words and Music by
HAL NEWMAN & RACHEL NEWMAN

THE BATTLE IS THE LORD'S

By STEVEN V. TAYLOR
& L. WAYNE HILLIARD

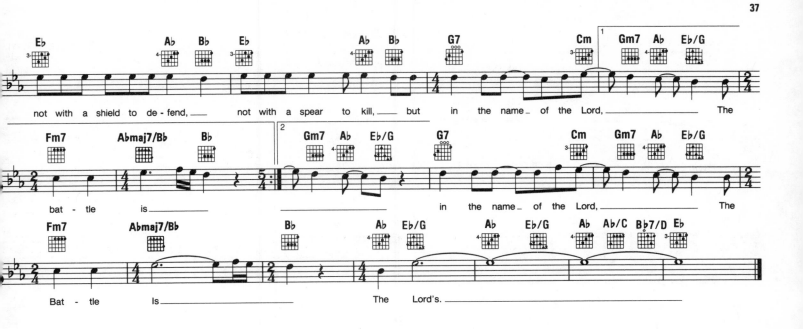

not with a shield to de-fend, ___ not with a spear to kill, ___ but in the name_ of the Lord, ___ The

bat-tle is ___ ___ in the name_ of the Lord, ___ The

Bat-tle Is ___ ___ The Lord's. ___

BORN AGAIN

By BARNEY T. SUDDERTH

Lively

1. I was a sin-ner. The Dev-il was in me. There was-n't room to let

2. (See additional lyrics)

___ sweet Je-sus in. Then I start-ed pray-in', and that's when He saved me.

Praise the name of Je-sus, I'm Born __ A-gain. I'm born (Born A- gain). ___ I'm born (Born A-

gain). ___ Je-sus died __ to save __ me from my __ sins. I'm born (Born A-

gain). ___ I'm born (Born A- gain). __ Like a lit-tle ba-by I'm Born __ A-gain. gain.

Additional Lyrics

2. It says in the Bible that Jesus is liable
To return any day. Are you ready for Him?
I wanna shout it. Tell all about it.
Glory Hallelujah, I'M BORN AGAIN.

Chorus

BATTLELINE

By TERI DeSARIO PURSE, BILL PUR
& DON CAS

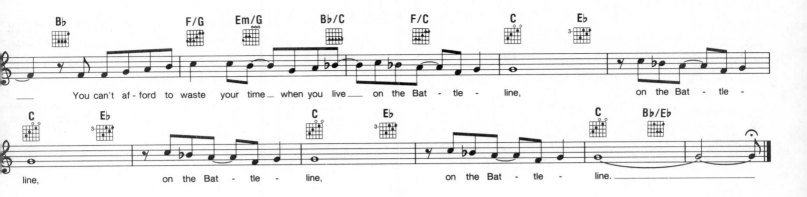

BELIEVERS

By PHILL McHUGH & JUSTIN PETERS

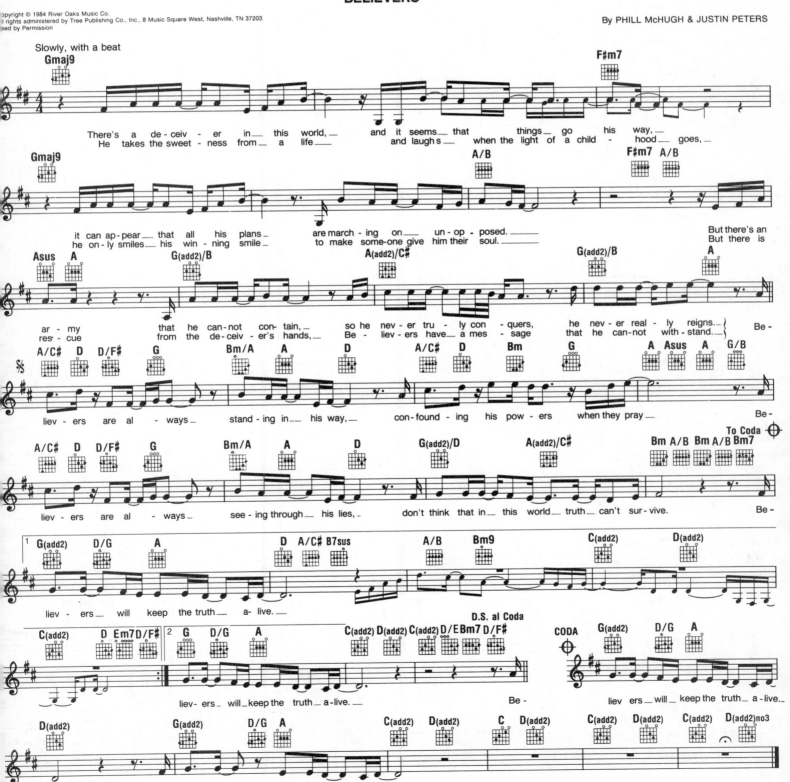

BARUCH HASHEM ADONAI

By DAWN RODGERS & TRICIA WALK

Moderately

VERSE

Who am I to be part of Your peo-ple The ones that are called by Your name? Could I be cho-sen a
How can a strang-er a rem-nant of na-tions Be-long to the roy-al line? You showed Your grace when th

CHORUS

one of Your own Could it be that our blood is the same? Ba-ruch ha-shem a-do-nai B
branch-es were bro-ken And I graft-ed in-to the Vine.

ruch ha-shem a-do-nai Bless-ed be the name of the Lord Ba-ruch ha-shem a-do-nai

3. How could You show me such bountiful mercy By taking the Life of the Lamb?
Your love is greater than I can imagine I bless You with all that I am.

4. Praise to You Jesus the veil has been parted And what once secret is known.
Now I can cry to You "Abba! My Father!" And praise You as one of Your own

BE STILL MY SOUL

By RUSS & TORI TA

Reverently

Sur-round-ed by the cares of life Sit-u-a-tions rise they press a-gainst my soul Des-perate thoughts have bloc
Teach me Lord to stay in You When my e-mo-tions try to rule me. Re-mind me Lord of

who I am Feels like I may lose con-trol A voice from some-where i
Show me what You want me to be. There is great strength

side of me brings com-fort fills my heart with cour-age And lets me know e-very-thing will be al-right
and con-fid-ence know-ing that You are with me I'm not a-fraid of tom-or-row what lies ahead

Be still my soul and know that He is God Stand qui-et-ly He is the Lord God is for me who can be a-gains

me Be still my soul He is the Lord

Be still my soul He is the Lord He is the Lord

BECAUSE OF WHO YOU ARE

By BILLY SMILEY & BOB FARRELL

BEHOLD THE LAMB

By DOTTIE RAMBO

BY MY SPIRIT

By LESLIE PHILLIPS

BELIEVING FOR THE BEST IN YOU

By MICHAEL & STORMIE OMARTIAN

BLESSED MESSIAH

By ED DeGARMO & DANA KEY

BLESSING

By PAM MARK HALL & GREG LAUGHER

BORN IN ZION

By MICHAEL HUDSON & GARY DRISKELL

Slowly with feeling

Ver-y few___ are born___ to rich-es,___ ver-y few.___
Ver-y few___ are ev-___ er fa-mous,___ ver-y few.___ at all.___

Ver-y few___ of cher-ished wish-es___ ev-er come___ true.___
Ver-y few___ will ev-___ er___ live___ the dream that they___ choose.___ But

that won't mat-ter much___ at all, ___ on the day your name___ is called,___ when this earth___ bound life___ is through.___

and___ your Fa-ther says___ of___ you. ___ This one___ was Born___ In Zion,

make no mis-take___ this one is mine.___ This one___ was Born___

3rd time to Coda

In Zi-on,___ this one will nev-er, this one will nev-er,

this one will nev-er die.___ this one will nev-er die.

And ev-'ry dream left un-ful-filled___ and ev-'ry wor-thy goal___

is just a sha-dow of___ the joy___ that waits___ for-ev-er to un-fold___

D.S. al Coda

CODA

this one will nev-er die.

BORN TO FLY

Words and Music by
CHARLES AARON WILBURN

BRAND NEW START

By AMY GRANT

BREAD UPON THE WATER

By BILL & JENNY GRE

CAN YOU REACH MY FRIEND

By BILLY SPRAGUE & JIM WEBER

With compassion, in "2"

I got a call ___ from an old ___ friend, ___ and I smiled when he men - tioned your name. ___ I
We talked for more ___ than an hour, ___ we laughed a - bout how ___ we had changed. ___

But I could tell ___ things weren't go - in' as well ___ as he claimed. He tried to hide ___ his feel -
said that I knew ___ you and told him the dif - f'rence you'd made. He nev - er thought ___ he would need

- ings, ___ but they on - ly gave ___ him a - way. The long - er I lis - tened, the
you, ___ but may - be he's chang - in' his mind. ___ As we said good - bye, Lord, he

more I kept wish - in' that I knew the right ___ words to say. ___ Can You Reach ___ My Friend?
told me that I had found some - thing that he'd like to ___ find.

___ You're the on - ly one ___ who can. ___ Lord I know ___ you love ___ him,

make him un - der - stand. ___ Can You Reach ___ My Friend, ___ bring his search - ing to ___ an end?

To Coda ⊕

Help him give ___ his heart ___ to You. ___ 'cause

may - be he's read - y to - night, Lord, he said ___ that he might ___ need to call ___ on You. ___

D.S. al Coda

CODA ⊕

to

you. ___ Help him give ___ his heart ___ to you. ___

CALVARY'S LOVE

By GREG NELSON & PHILL McHU...

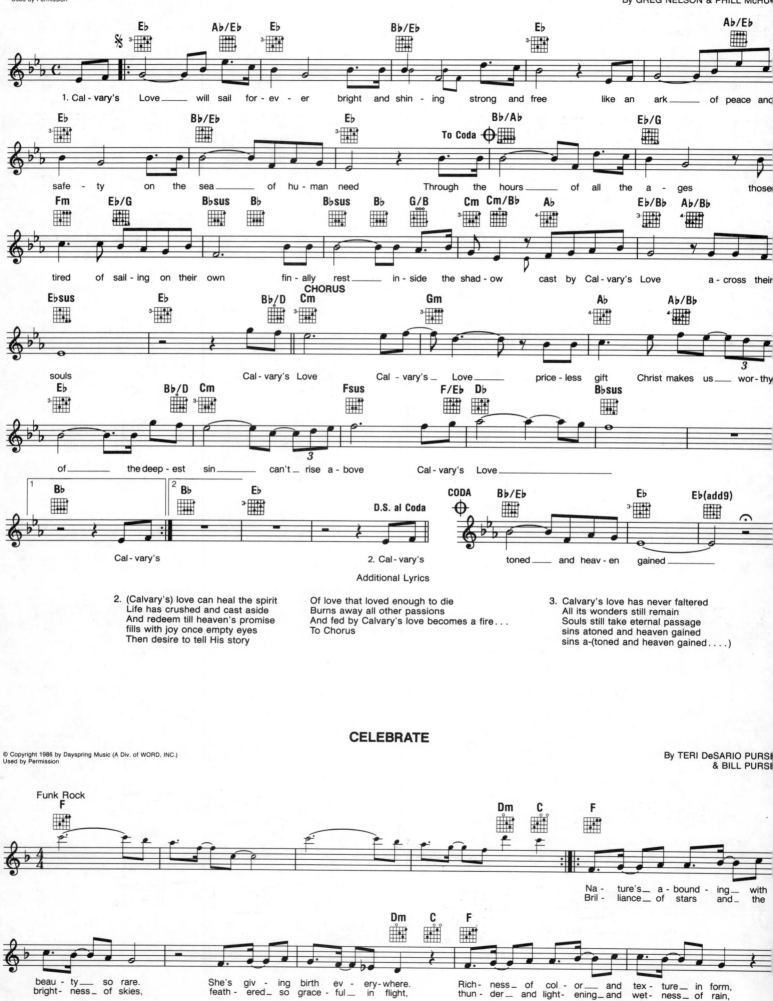

1. Cal-vary's Love will sail for-ev-er bright and shin-ing strong and free like an ark of peace and safe-ty on the sea of hu-man need Through the hours of all the a-ges those tired of sail-ing on their own fin-ally rest in-side the shad-ow cast by Cal-vary's Love a-cross their souls

CHORUS

Cal-vary's Love Cal-vary's Love price-less gift Christ makes us wor-thy of the deep-est sin can't rise a-bove Cal-vary's Love

Cal-vary's 2. Cal-vary's

D.S. al Coda

CODA

toned and heav-en gained

Additional Lyrics

2. (Calvary's) love can heal the spirit
Life has crushed and cast aside
And redeem till heaven's promise
fills with joy once empty eyes
Then desire to tell His story

Of love that loved enough to die
Burns away all other passions
And fed by Calvary's love becomes a fire...
To Chorus

3. Calvary's love has never faltered
All its wonders still remain
Souls still take eternal passage
sins atoned and heaven gained
sins a-(toned and heaven gained....)

CELEBRATE

By TERI DeSARIO PURS...
& BILL PURS...

Funk Rock

Na-ture's a-bound-ing with beau-ty so rare. She's giv-ing birth ev-ery-where. Rich-ness of col-or and tex-ture in form,
Bril-liance of stars and the bright-ness of skies, feath-ered so grace-ful in flight, thun-der and light-ening and wet-ness of rain,

CELEBRATE HIS GOOD LIFE

By JOHN ELLIOTT, GREG NELSON
MICHAEL W. SMITH & STEVE GREEN

1. We will cel - e - brate___ our gra - cious Lord___ Though He was rich made Him - self poor Like no

2. (see additional lyrics)

oth - er king___ the world___ had known be - fore___ Through His pov - er - ty___ we have re - ceived___ an

ov - er - flow___ that longs___ to reach in - to ev - ery need___ and fill___ it joy - ful - ly___ We will

CHORUS

Cel - e - brate___ His Good Life___ We will cel - e - brate___ with joy We will cel - e - brate___ His life___ We will

cel - e - brate___ with joy Cel - e - brate___ our Lord's good___ life

Additional Lryics

2. Let us celebrate our gracious Lord
Who teaches us to give Him more
Than we ever dreamed that we could give before
For we have become the cheeful ones
Who find our joy when His will is done
And in loving all there's life that overcomes

Chorus

CELEBRATION

Words and Music by SHIRLEY CAESAR WILLIAMS
& BERNARD STERLING

Cel - e - bra - tion, ju - bi - la - tion. Cel - e - bra - tion_____ ju - bi

- la - tion. We're gon - na have a great Cel - e - bra - tion_____ of the
- len - ni - al reign is gon - na sure - ly come_____ and then

55

THE CHAMPION

By CARMAN LICCIARDELLO

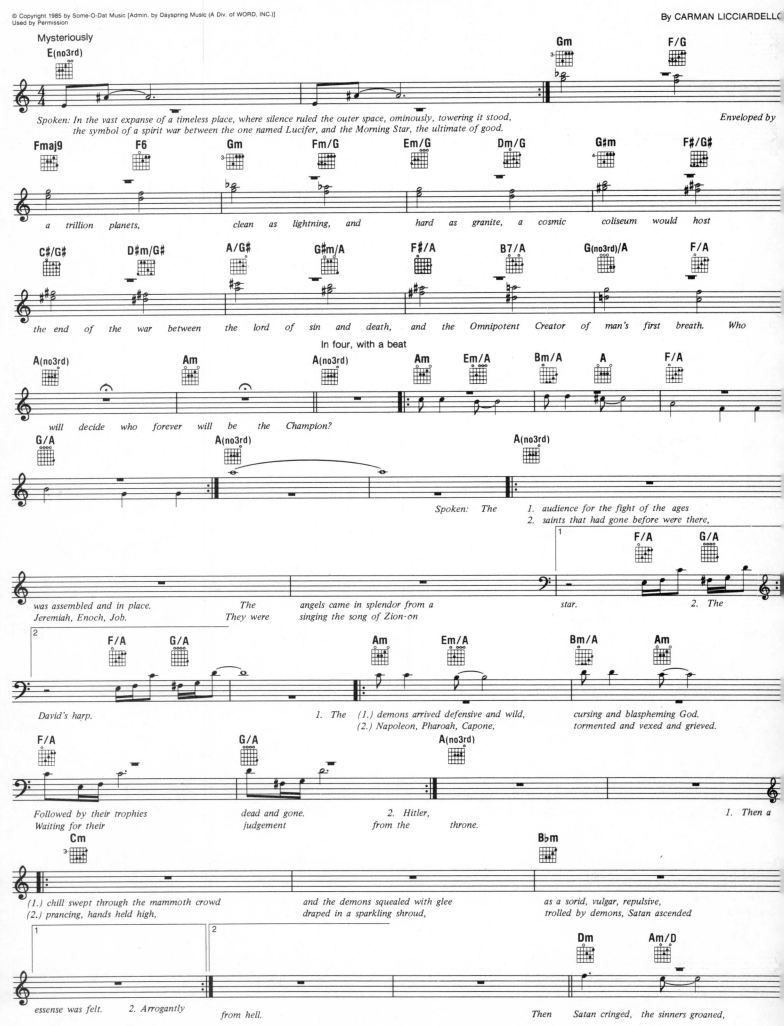

Spoken: In the vast expanse of a timeless place, where silence ruled the outer space, ominously, towering it stood, the symbol of a spirit war between the one named Lucifer, and the Morning Star, the ultimate of good. Enveloped by

a trillion planets, clean as lightning, and hard as granite, a cosmic coliseum would host

the end of the war between the lord of sin and death, and the Omnipotent Creator of man's first breath. Who

will decide who forever will be the Champion?

Spoken: The 1. audience for the fight of the ages
2. saints that had gone before were there,

was assembled and in place. The angels came in splendor from a star. 2. The
Jeremiah, Enoch, Job. They were singing the song of Zion-on

David's harp. 1. The (1.) demons arrived defensive and wild, cursing and blaspheming God.
(2.) Napoleon, Pharoah, Capone, tormented and vexed and grieved.

Followed by their trophies dead and gone. 2. Hitler, 1. Then a
Waiting for their judgement from the throne.

(1.) chill swept through the mammoth crowd and the demons squealed with glee as a sorid, vulgar, repulsive,
(2.) prancing, hands held high, draped in a sparkling shroud, trolled by demons, Satan ascended

essense was felt. 2. Arrogantly from hell. Then Satan cringed, the sinners groaned,

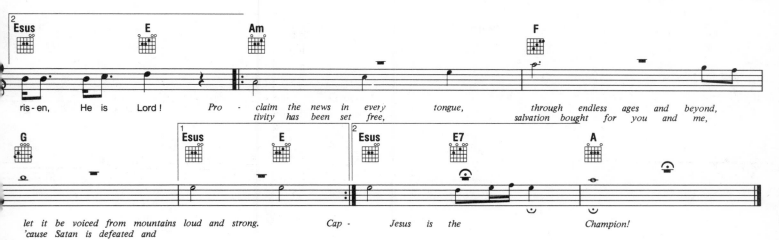

Esus   **E**   **Am**   **F**

ris - en, He is Lord !   *Pro - claim the news in every tongue,*   *through endless ages and beyond,*
tivity has been set free,   *salvation bought for you and me,*

G   **Esus**   **E**   **Esus**   **E7**   **A**

let it be voiced from mountains loud and strong.   *Cap -*   Jesus is the   Champion!
'cause Satan is defeated and

CORNERSTONE

By LEON PATILLO

Majestically **Cm**   **Fm**   **G**   **Cm**

I lay in Zi - on for a foun - da - tion of stone I lay in Zi - on for a foun -

Fm   **G**   **Fm**   **Bb7**   **Eb**   **Ab**   **Dm7**   **G7**   **Cm**   **G7**   **Cm**

da - tion of stone a tried stone a pre-cious cor - ner - stone a sure foun - da - tion a sure foun - da - tion tion a

Fm   **Bb7**   **Eb**   **Ab**   **Dm7**   **G7**   **Cm**   **C**

tried stone a pre - cious cor - ner - stone he that be - liev - eth shall, shall not make haste Won - der - ful

Bb   **Ab**   **Bb**   **C**

Coun - sel - or the might - y God the e - ver - last - ing Fa - ther Won - der - ful

Bb   **Fm7**   **Gm7**   **Ab**   **[1,2]**   **[3] Abmaj7**   **C**

Coun - sel - or the Prince of Peace. Won - der - ful,

Bb   **Ab**   **Bb**   **C**

Coun - sel - or, the might - y God the e - ver - last - ing Fa - ther. Won - der - ful,

Bb   **Fm7**   **Gm7**   **Abmaj7**   **Fm7**   **Gm7**   **Abmaj7**   **Fm7**   **Gm7**   **Abmaj7**   **Bb**   **C**

Coun - sel - or, the Prince of Peace Prince of Peace Prince of Peace.

CELEBRATE THE LORD

By JOHN ELLIOTT & MARK BALDW

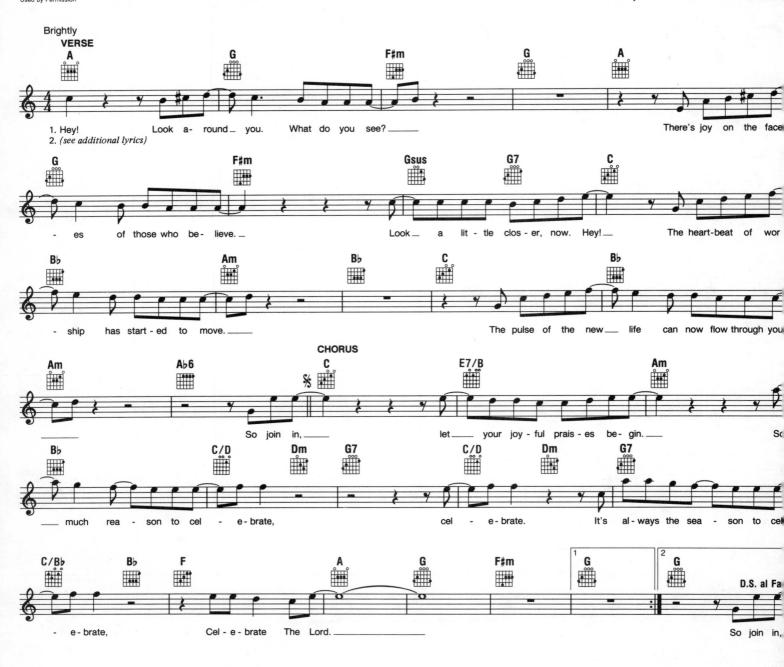

Additional Lyrics

2. Hey! Look inside you.
What do you see?
Do you find joy in what you believe?
Look a little closer, now.
Hey! Is your heart keepin' time
with the spirit of praise?
Are you hopin' to climb
to a much higher place?
Now's the time to...

Chorus

CHAMPION OF THE BATTLE

By JACK FOWLER & JAMES SIGMON

CHRIST THE LORD IS RISEN TODAY

By CHARLES WESLEY & MICHAEL W. SM

CHORUS

O Christ the Lord is ris - en. Christ The Lord Is Ris - en To - day, al - le -

lu - ia. Sons of men __ and __ an - gels say al - le - lu - ia, al -

- le - lu - ia. __ - ia. O Christ the Lord is ris - en. __

CONVERSATION PEACE

Words and Music by
CHARLES AARON WILBURN

Quickly

I could sing a - bout the wea - ther or pla - ces that I've been, the all the things
If I don't seem to get ex - ci - ted a - bout the la - test news, the win - ning teams or

I have plans to do, but there's a peace that I've been giv - en, since I gave my heart to
wars that just broke out, if my con - ver - sa - tion seems to lead to Him, it's just be -

Him; and that's what I'd real - ly like to share with you. It's a Con - ver - sa - tion Peace, peace be -
cause I've found some - thing I just love to talk about.

yond my un - der - stand - ing; I __ love to tell what He's done for me. __ It's a feel - ing I can't

hide, I can't keep it down in - side; the peace of God is a con - ver - sa - tion peace.

CIRCLE OF TWO

Words and Music
MICKEY CA...

Additional Lyrics

2. There's time for the working
Time for the play
There never seems to be enough time to pray
But let's put the past behind us
We can start again tonight
Just sit by me — hold my hand
We will make it right
For he delights...

COME AND SEE

By BOB BENNETT & MICHAEL AGUILAR

THE COLORING SONG

Words and Musi
DAVE E

1. Red is the col-or of the blood that flowed down the face of some-one who loved us so. He's the per-fect man, He's the Lord's own Son, He's
2. Blue is the col-or of a heart so cold that will not bend when the sto-ry's told of the love of God for a sin-ful race, of

Lamb of God He's the on-ly one that can give us life, that can make us grow, that can make the love be- tween us
blood that flowed down Je-sus' face that can give us life, that can make us grow, that can keep our hearts from grow-ing

flow.
cold.

snow. That can give us life, that can make us grow, {that ca
{that ca

turn our morn-ings in- to gold. That can
keep our hearts from grow-ing cold. That can
make the love be- tween us

flow.

3. Gold is the color of the morning sun that shines so freely on everyone. It's the sun of love that keeps us warm, it's the sun of love that calms the storm, that can give us life, that can give us life that can make us grow, that can turn our mourning into gold.

4. Brown is the color of the autumn leaves when then winter comes to the barren trees. Th is birth, there is death, there is a plan, and there's just one God, and there's just one ma that can give us life, that can make us grow, that can make our sins as white as snow.

COME TO THE TABLE

Words and Music
NILES BOROP & MICHAEL CA

Come To The Ta- ble and sa- vor the sight, the wine and the bread that was
Come To The Ta- ble and see in His eyes the love that the Fath- er has

bro- ken. And all have been wel- come to come if they might, ac-cept as their own
spo- ken. And know you are wel- come what-ev- er your crime, though e- ery com-man

these two to- kens. The bread is His bod- y, the wine is His blood,
- ment you've bro-ken. For He's come to love you and not to con- demn, and the

COME CELEBRATE JESUS

By CLAIRE CLONINGER & JOHN ROSA

VERSE

1. The door is o - pen wide and on the hearth a fire is burn - ing
2. *(See additional lyrics)*

The rooms are full of light the fes - tive meal has been pre - pared and the

song in - vites you in to come share your life with Him Come cel - e - brate

CHORUS

Je - sus Come Cel - e - brate Je - sus the bread and the wine

the mo - ment in time Come Cel - e - brate Je - sus the spir - it that frees us

His ta - ble has been laid come now and Cel - e - brate

Him Let it start

Let it be - gin Lift up your heart

Cel - e - brate Him cel - e - brate Him

Additional Lyrics

2. He is the open door
He is the fire that welcomes and crowns us
He is the song of joy
That leads a hungry heart back home
For his life's the melody
And his love the victory
Chorus

COUNT THE COST

By RANDY L. SCRUGGS
& JOHN W. THOMPSON

COUNT ME IN

By JOHN W. THOMPS
MICHAEL CARD & RANDY L. SCRUG

Joyfully
CHORUS

When you num-ber _ the ones who be-lieve in Him, Count me in, Count me in; When they o-pen _ the gates to Je-ru-sa-lem, Count

Fine VERSE

in, Count me in.
What a day that will be when He comes for you and me, When we gath-er on the oth-er
How our fac-es will shine as we stand _ in the line that leads us to our home a-

side. What a joy we will share with our loved ones _ there, Where we will for-ev-er a-bide.
bove. Ev-'ry tear will be dried as we stand in the Light Of His ev-er-last-ing love.

THE DARKNESS IS UNDER HIS FEET

Words and Music
TANYA GOODMAN & DAVID BINI

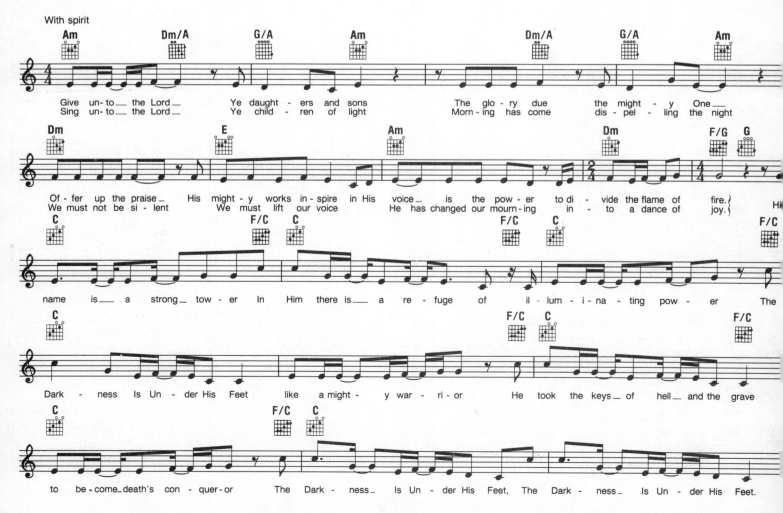

With spirit

Give un-to _ the Lord _ Ye daught-ers and sons The glo-ry due the might-y One _
Sing un-to _ the Lord _ Ye child-ren of light Morn-ing has come dis-pel-ling the night

Of-fer up the praise _ His might-y works in-spire in His voice _ is the pow-er to di-vide the flame of fire.
We must not be si-lent We must lift our voice He has changed our mourn-ing in-to a dance of joy.

name is a strong _ tow-er In Him there is _ a re-fuge of il-lum-i-na-ting pow-er The

Dark-ness Is Un-der His Feet like a might-y war-ri-or He took the keys _ of hell _ and the grave

to be-come _ death's con-quer-or The Dark-ness _ Is Un-der His Feet, The Dark-ness _ Is Un-der His Feet.

THE DARKER THE NIGHT

By MICHAEL JAMES MURPHY

THE DAY HE WORE MY CROWN

By PHIL JOHNS

1. The ci-ty was Je-ru-sa-lem; The time was long a-go. The peo-ple called Hi
2. He brought me love that on-ly He could give; I brought Him cause to cry. And though He taught m

Je - sus, the crime was the love He showed. And I'm the one to blame; I caused all th
how to live I taught Him how to die.

pain. He gave Him-self _____ the day He wore _____ my crown. _____ my crown. _____

_____ my crown. _____ He could have called _ His Ho-ly Fa-ther_ and said, "Take me a-way, please _ take me a-way." He could have said_ "I'm n

gui - ty, _____ and I'm not gon-na stay, I'm not gon-na pay." _____ _____ my crown. I'm the one to blame.

I caused all the pain. He gave Him-self _____ the day He wore _____ my crown. _____

3. But He walked right through the gate; And then on up the hill.
And as He fell beneath the weight, He cried, "Father, not my will."

DESTINED TO WIN

By ED DeGARMO & DANA K

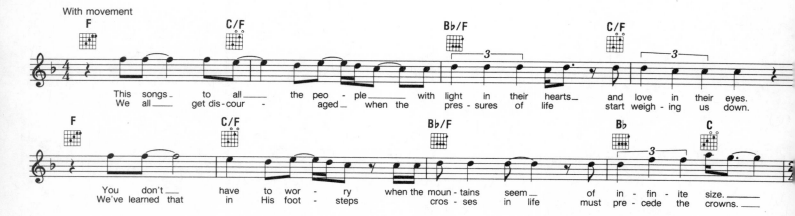

This songs_ to all _ the peo - ple with light in their hearts_ and love in their eyes.
We all _____ get dis-cour - aged when the pres-sures of life start weigh-ing us down.

You don't _ have to wor - ry when the moun-tains seem of in - fin - ite size._
We've learned that in His foot-steps cros-ses in life must pre-cede the crowns._

DO I TRUST YOU

By TWILA PARIS

DOER OF THE WORD

By JEREMY DALTON

DO SOMETHING NOW

By STEVE CAMP & PHIL MADEIR

DON'T LOOK BACK

Words and Music
TANYA GOODMAN & TERRY TOL

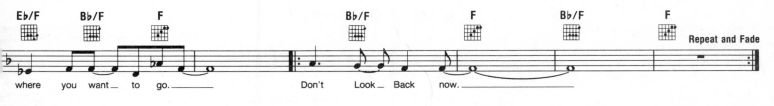

DON'T RUN AWAY

By AMY GRANT & GARY CHAPMAN

DRAWIN' FROM THE WELL

By PHIL JOHNS

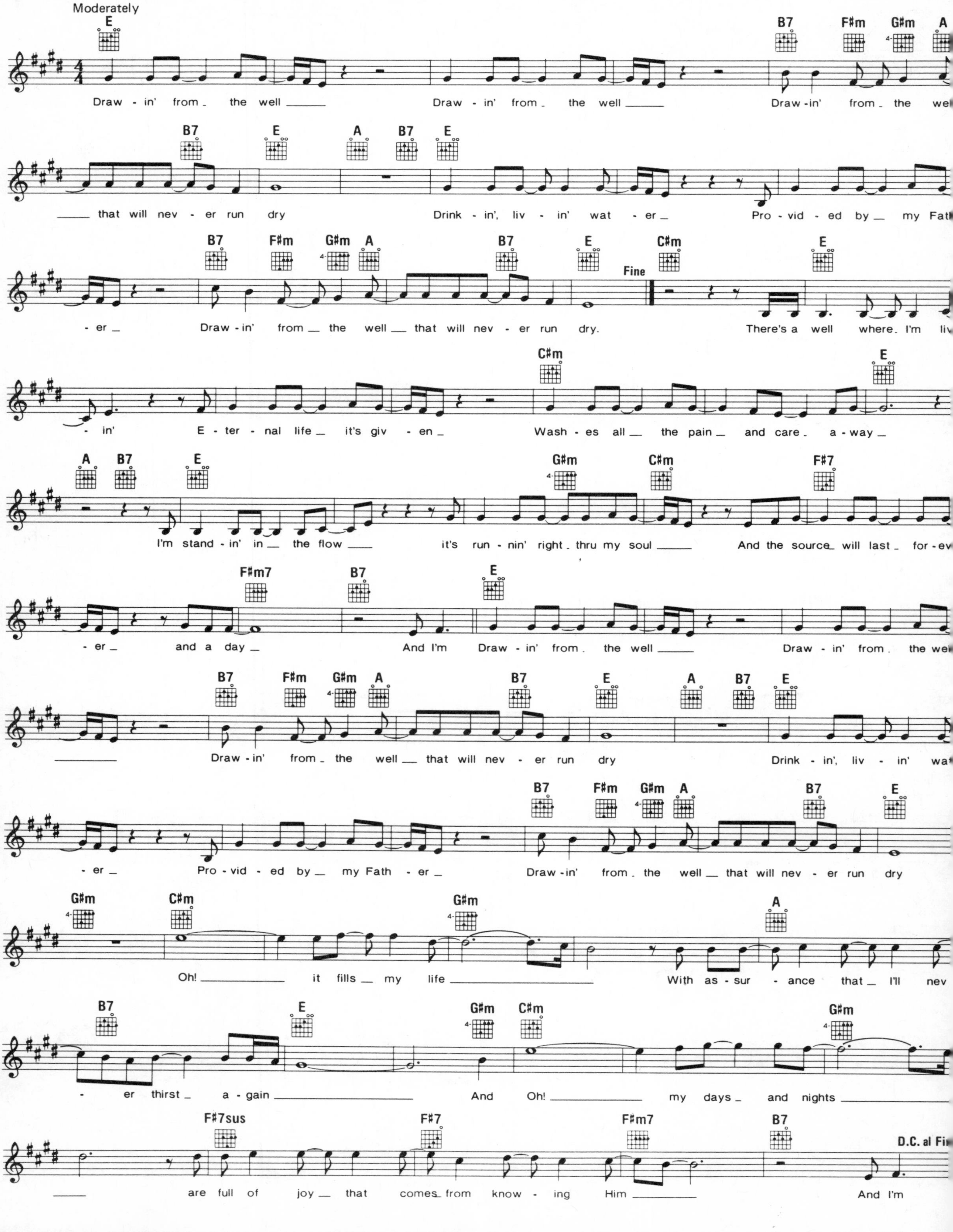

EAGLE SONG

By RUSS & TORI TAFF

3. I reached for the eternal one creation He was waiting to reveal His purpose in me. He said, "this is where life begins - I made your spirit to light on the wind."

Doubly Good To You

By RICHARD MULLI

Fervently

If you see the morn - ing ris - ing gent - ly on ___ your fields ___ If the wind blow soft - ly on ___ your fa

___ and if the sun-set lin - gers ___ while ca-the-dral bells peal ___ and the moon has ris - en to ___ her

place You can thank the Fath - er ___ for the things ___ that He has done and thank Him for the things ___ he's yet ___ to do

And if you find a love that's ten - der ___ and if you find some - one who's true ___ then thank the Lord

___ He's been Dou - bl - y Good ___ To You ___ If you look in the mir - ror at th

end of a ___ hard day ___ and you know in your ___ heart you ___ have not lied ___ and if you gave love free - ly ___ if yo

earned an hon - est wage and if you've got Je - sus on ___ your side You can thank the Fath - er ___ for the th

___ that He has done and thank Him for the things ___ he's yet ___ to do ___ And if you find a love that's ten - der ___ and if yo

find some - one who's true ___ then thank the Lord ___ He's been Dou - bl - y Good ___ To You

You can thank the Fath - er ___ for the things ___ that He has done and thank Him for the things ___ he's yet ___ to do ___ And if you

find a love that's ten - der___ and if you find some - one who' true___ then thank the Lord___ He's been Dou - bl - y Good _ To You___

___ Thank the Lord___ He's been Dou - bl - y Good _ To You___

EASTER SONG

By ANNE HERRING

973 Latter Rain Music

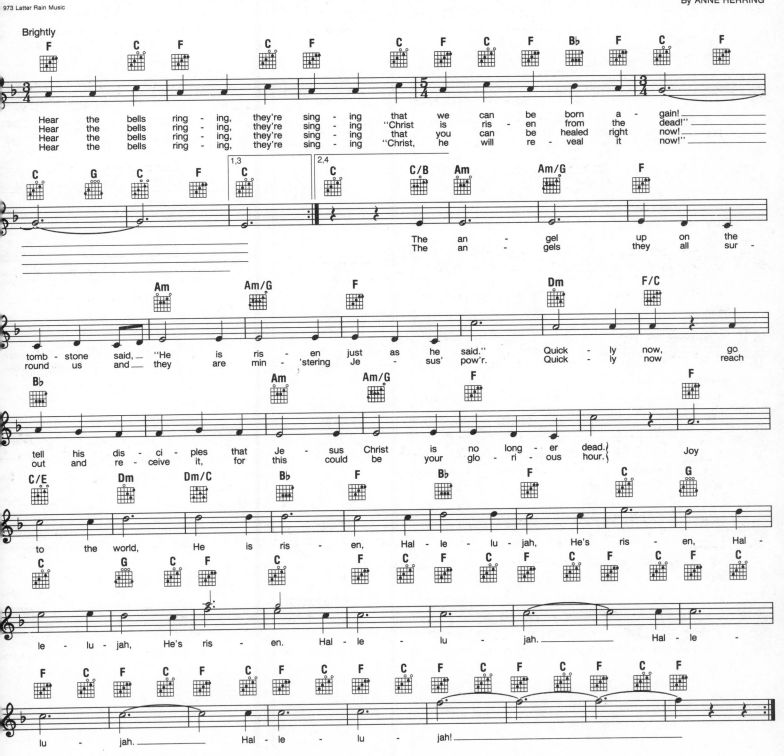

Brightly

Hear the bells ring - ing, they're sing - ing that we can be born a - gain! ___
Hear the bells ring - ing, they're sing - ing "Christ is ris - en born from the dead!" ___
Hear the bells ring - ing, they're sing - ing that you can be healed right now! ___
Hear the bells ring - ing, they're sing - ing "Christ, he will re - veal it now!" ___

The an - gel up on the
The an - gels they all sur -

tomb - stone said, ___ "He is ris - en just as he said." Quick - ly now, go
round us and ___ they are min - 'stering Je - sus' pow'r. Quick - ly now reach

tell his dis - ci - ples that Je - sus Christ is no long - er dead.) Joy
out and re - ceive it, for this could be your glo - ri - ous hour.}

to the world, He is ris - en, Hal - le - lu - jah, He's ris - en, Hal

le - lu - jah, He's ris - en. Hal - le - lu - jah. ___ Hal - le -

lu - jah. ___ Hal - le - lu - jah! ___

END OF THE BOOK

By MICHAEL W. SMITH & MIKE HUDSON

EVERY STEP OF THE WAY

By NAN GURLEY, JIM WEBER
& BILLY SPRAGUE

With conviction

When the road is long and hard, And I think I'm on ___ my own; Then His Spir-it,
When my cour-age dis-ap-pears, He will put His hand ___ in mine; For He prom-ised ___

in my heart, Tells me I am not a-lone, ___ Ev-'ry Step Of The Way ___ my Fa-ther
to be here, e-ven to the end of time. ___

leads, He is all the strength, ___ I need to go on from day to day. ___ I know that some-day I will

see what He's work-ing out ___ in me, Ev-'ry Step Of The Way. ___ me, Ev-'ry Step Of The Way.

I don't know if to-mor-row will bring me joy or pain.

I on-ly know ___ when I lift ___ my heart to pray, ___ He is nev-er far a-

way. ___ Ev-'ry Step Of The Way ___ my Fa-ther leads, ___

___ He is all the strength ___ I need to go on ___ from day to day. I know that some-day I will see ___

___ what He's work-in' out ___ in me, Ev-'ry Step Of The Way. ___ Ev-'ry Step Of The Way, ___

Ev-'ry Step Of The Way. ___

EL SHADDAI

By JOHN W. THOMPS[...]
& MICHAEL CA[...]

Slow 2-Gentle Feel

CHORUS

El Shad-dai, __ El Shad-dai, __ El El-yon na A - don-ai, __ Age to ag[...]

__ You're still the same__ by the pow - er of __ the name; El Shad-dai, __ El Shad-dai, __ er - kam-k[...]

__ na A - don-ai __ We will praise and lift __ You __ high, El Shad-dai. __ high, El Shad-da[...]

Fine __ El Shad-dai.

VERSES

Thru Your love __ and thru __ the ram You saved the son __ of A - bra-ha[...]
Thru the years __ You made __ it clear That the time __ of Christ __ was ne[...]

Thru the pow - er of __ Your __ hand Turned the sea __ in - to __ dry __ land; To the out[...]
Tho' the peo - ple could - n't see __ What Mes - si - ah ought to __ be; Tho' Your W[...]

- cast on __ her knees __ You were the God __ who real - ly sees: __ and by Your might __ You set Your chil - dren
con - tained __ the plan They just could not un - der - stand:

free. __ Your most awe - some work __ was done __ Thru the frail - ty of __ Your Son.

ELIJAH

By RICHARD MULLIN[...]

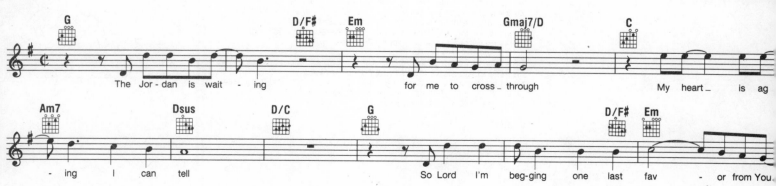

The Jor - dan is wait - ing for me to cross __ through My heart __ is ag[...]

- ing I can tell So Lord I'm beg-ging one last fav - or from You

Additional Lyrics

2. There's people been friendly but they'd never be your friend
Sometimes this has bent me to the ground
But now that this is all ending I want to hear my music once again
'Cause it's the finest thing that I have ever found
Now the Jordan is waiting and I ain't never seen the other side
But I know I can't take in what I have here

On the road to salvation I stick out my thumb and He gives me a ride
And this music is already falling on my ear
There's people been talking, they say they're worried about my soul
Well, I'm here to tell you I'll keep rocking 'til I'm sure it's
my time to roll, and when I do...

Chorus

EMMANUEL

By MICHAEL W. SMITH

EVERYWHERE I GO

Words and Music by
MARYLEE KORTE

89

EVENING SONG

Words and Mus
WILLIAM RICHARD

THE EXODUS SONG

Words by PAT BOO
Music by ERNEST GO

FAIREST OF TEN THOUSAND

Words and Music by TANYA GOODMAN
DAVID R. LEHMAN & MICHAEL SYKES

FAITH TAKES A VISION

By JAMES W.

FAITH WALKIN' PEOPLE

By BROWN BANNISTER & AMY GRANT

FAN MAIL

Words and Music by
MICKI FUHRMAN & TANYA GOODM...

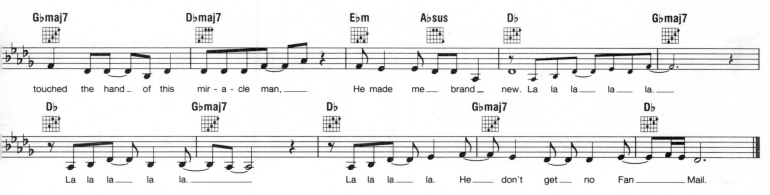

touched the hand of this mir-a-cle man, He made me brand new. La la la la la la.

La la la la la. La la la la. He don't get no Fan Mail.

FINALLY

By GARY CHAPMAN

Moderately

I wish my mind would-n't ar - gue with my heart It splits the day a - part In - to time
fer - ris wheel just keeps on spin - nin' 'round Play - in' mind games with the ground. Can we stop

well spent and time just thrown a - way. I wish my heart would please make up my mind
this time or must we go a - gain? I see You stand - ing wait - ing just out - side

Wast - in' so much time Got - ta catch a glimpse of what I'm gon - na be
Come and get me off this ride, Want - a lose my - self in be - ing there with You

CHORUS

When fin - al - ly I look in - side Your eyes and see Re-

flec - tions of Your - self in me The way You al - ways said it'd be When fin-

- al - ly I'm lov - in' You like You love me It hap - pened oh so eas - i - ly I

looked at You it came to me fin - al - ly

This

FATHER'S EYES

By GARY CHAPM

FIND A HURT AND HEAL IT

By DAVID BARONI
& NILES BOROP

FIND A WAY

By MIKE HUDS
& MICHAEL W. SM

through? Love _____ will Find A Way, love ___ will Find A Way. I know ___ it's hard to see the past ___ and still be-lieve, love ___ is gon-na Find A Way _____ Love ___ will Find A Way, love ___ will make a way. Leave ___ **Repeat and Fade** be-hind your doubt, loves ___ the on-ly out, love ___ will sure-ly Find A Way. ___ Love ___

FOR THE LOVE OF IT

Copyright 1981 by Fifty Grand Music, Inc. (BMI), 50 Music Square West, Nashville, TN 37203

Words and Music by
JERRY MICHAEL & KATHLEEN MURDOCK

A new be-gin-ning much more than a chance ___ Learn-ing 'bout new love and leav-ing the past ___
I found a place ___ with Je-sus my friend, ___ A world of rain-bows where love nev-er ends, ___

Luck-y for me ___ Your love has o-pened _____ my eyes ___ Now I re-a-lize; ___
Sing-ing His name ___ with hearts ___ in His hands. He al-ways ___ un-der-stands; ___

CHORUS

Just for the love ___ of it thru His eyes we see ___ Just for the love ___ of it, it works per-fect-ly ___ A-long with His wis-dom we

D.C. al Coda **CODA**

have all we need Shar-ing His love ___ so gen-'rous-ly ___ He gave us each oth - er.

THE FIRST STONE

By GEOFF THURMAN, BECKY THUR...
& JUSTIN PE...

With movement

VERSE

She was led there for con-dem-na-tion   They knew her fate was now in-sured   As

2. (see additional lyrics)

heard ev-'ry ac-cu-sa-tion   Her shame and her guilt en-dured   They knew death was the right sol-u-

-tion   But the Lord had an-oth-er plan   Take a-way their right-eous il-lu-sion   Teach ...

CHORUS

pas-sion to ev-'ry man   You are her ac-cus-ers   You try to a-buse her   You don't know the Ho-ly On...

Who of you is wor-thy   Who will see His glo-ry   Who will throw The First Stone

1. C/E D/E   2. C/E D/E

throw The First Stone.   2. There are

Additional lyrics

VS 2/   There are none of us here so righteous
        That our lives are not marred by sin
        Our vain strivings become so pious
        We lose touch with the grace within

        Jesus cries for our heartless anger
        He once bled just to pay the price
        We forget how we once refused love
        How we saw life with blinded eyes...(to CHO 2)

CHO 2/ We are the accusers
        We are the abusers
        We think we're the holy ones
        Who of us is worthy
        Who will see the glory
        Who will throw the first stone, throw the first stone...(Rpt.)

FOREVER

By CLAIRE CLONINGER & JOHN ROSA...

Smoothly

1. Sun-sets and seas-ons and streams   like our dreams come and go
2,3. (See additional lyrics)

But He is the peace in our lives   that sur-vived

Additional Lyrics

2. Mountains may crumble and fall after all what are they
But He is the joy that endures-we are sure He will stay

Chorus He is Forever and ever
What time can't destroy
He is the song of joy
He is Forever and ever
What time can't destroy
Our never ending everlasting joy

3. We are like castles of sand___now we stand___now we're gone
But He is is the love that remains___tho we change___He goes on

Chorus He is Forever and ever
Our Father above___He is the heart of our love
He is Forever and ever
Our father above___our never ending___everlasting love

FLAWLESS

By JIM WEBER, GEOFF THURM
& BECKY THURM

FOLLOWING THE KING

By MARK GERSMEHL & BILLY SMILEY

Bright Gospel Rock

He nev-er told us pret-ty stor-ies___ He did-n't try to feed us shin-y lies.
hold us up as he-roes___ cuz the pow-er that we have is not our own___

He said the way of faith_ was-n't eas-y And the world would make_ it hard-er all the time.___
for the strength that is___ in-side_ us is com-ing from_ the one who leads us home.___

But we've heard his truth___ And made___ our choice,___ We know where we___ are go-___ing,
Spir-it of love,___ He is___ our source___ He shows us where_ we're go-___ing,

We're not turn-ing back or chang-ing course;___ } We are march-ing___ on Fol-low-ing The King. We are his peo-
We're not turn-ing back or chang-ing course;___ }

-ple___ We will go where he leads.___ We are march-ing___ on Sing-ing songs of vic- to-ry. We're get-ting strong-

-er. So much strong-er___ We are Fol-low-ing___ The King___

Don't you ___ We be-lieve___ in the King___ of Kings.___ We be-lieve

**Repeat and Fade
and ad lib Vocal**

We are march-ing___ on Fol-low-ing___ The King_____

Following You

Words and Music by
LISA HARPER & LAURIE HARPER

Wan - dering a - bout _____ trou - bled with doubt _____ life just hap - pens _____ that way _____ A - midst the com - mo - tion _____ touched _____ with e - mo - tion _____ then came the no - tion to pray. Can You hear _____ my cry _____ I want _____ to try _____ to live my life for You _____ I am one _____ who comes _____ as a child _____ to fol - low You. Fol - low - ing You _____ Fol - low - ing You. My Lord _____ I am one _____ who comes _____ as a child to fol - low You. _____ Fol - low - ing one _____ who comes _____ as a child to fol - low You. _____ Which path shall I take, will it be a mis - take Ques - tions I need an - swers to. _____ Great _____ ex - pec - ta - tions _____ fa - cing re - ject - ions Need - ing di - rect - ions _____ from You _____ Fol - low - ing

FOR UNTO US

By MELODIE TUNNEY, DICK TUNNEY
& BEVERLY DARNALL

Additional lyrics

2. Love and goodwill,
The Creator in mercy
Takes His own life in His hands,
Places this life in the Savior, a baby
Who is God and yet He is a man.

(Chorus)

FORGIVEN

By DAVID MEE

FRIENDLY FIRE

Words and Music by
TANYA GOODMAN & DAVID BINION

FRIENDS

By MICHAEL W. SMI'
& DEBORAH D. SMI'

FROM THIS MOMENT

Words and Music by
LISA HARPER

Stately

1. From This Mo-ment I ded-i-cate _ my life to you From This
2. (See additional lyrics)
Mo-ment the sun has bro-ken through _____ free as an ea-gle to fly _____
_ in the strength _ of your love I've wait-ed so long _ now _ my
fear _ is gone your grace re- leased me From This Mo-ment chains no long-er _ bind _
From This Mo-ment _ I leave the past be- hind _____ From This
Mo-ment _ new life in you I _ find.
From This Mo-ment, From this _ ver-y mo- ment, mo- ment.

Repeat and Fade

Additional Lyrics

2. From This Moment
   No rain can cloud my day
   From This Moment
   No wrong can make me stray
   I'm like the lily
   Determined to grow
   In your care
   Your guiding light
   Will show me the right
   You'll always be there

FORGIVING EYES

By MICHAEL CA[...]
& NORBERT PUTN[...]

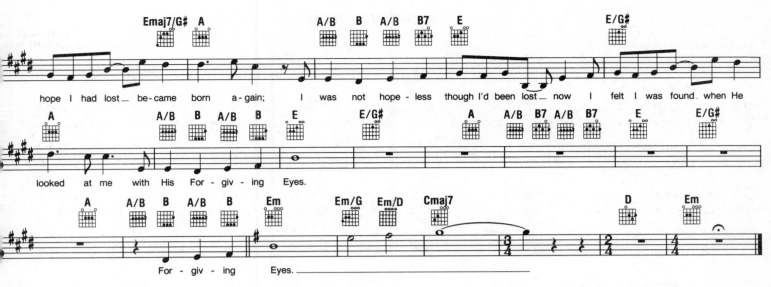

hope I had lost_ be-came born a-gain; I was not hope-less though I'd been lost_ now I felt I was found. when He

looked at me with His For-giv-ing Eyes.

For - giv - ing Eyes. _____

GOD'S WONDERFUL PEOPLE

By LANNY WOLFE

CHORUS

Moderately

1,2. I love the thrill that I feel when I get to-geth-er with God's won-der-ful peo-ple,_ Love the thrill that I feel when I

get to-geth-er with God's won-der-ful peo-ple._ What a sight just to see all the hap-py fac-es_ Prais-ing God, in

Heav-en-ly plac-es, What a thrill that I feel when I get to-geth-er with God's _____ won-der-ful peo-ple.

Fine VERSE

Oh, what joy His love af-fords_ when we meet in one ac-cord,_ And we lift our hearts in
It can be just an-y-where_ two or three are gath-ered there. That the Spir-it of the

praise_ un-to the Lord; _____ There's no place I'd rath-er__ be than_ with the ones who've been set_
Lord_ will be there, too._ There's no fel-low-ship so_ sweet,_ there's no thrill that can com-

1.
2.
D.S. al Fine

free; I'm so glad I'm in God's_ great big fam-i-ly.__ I love the
pete With the thrill I feel when-ev-er God's chil-dren meet. I love the

3. On that great reunion day when our Lord says "Come away,"
And the saints from every land sweet through the gates.
Joining loved ones 'round the throne, at last we'll all be gathered home.
That will be the greatest thrill we've ever known.

GIVE THEM ALL TO JESUS

By PHIL JOHNSON & BOB BEN

Are you tired of chas-in' _____ pret-ty rain-bows, and are you tired of spin-nin' 'round a
He nev-er said _____ you'd on-ly _____ see sun-shine, and He _____ nev-er said _____ there'd be

'round? ___ Wrap up all the shat-tered dreams of _____ your life _____ and at the feet of Je-
rain. He _____ on-ly prom-ised a heart full of sing-ing _____ a-bout the ver-y thing

CHORUS

-sus. lay them down. } Give them all, give them all, _____ give them all _ to
that once brought pain.

-sus. Shat-tered dreams, wound-ed hearts_ and bro-ken toys; _____ Give them all, give them all, ___

give them all _ to Je-sus. And He will turn _ your sor-row in-to joy. _____

GOD'S OWN FOOL

By MICHAEL C.

It seems I've im-ag-ined Him all of my_____ life as the wis-est of all_____ of man-kind; but

God's ho-ly wis-dom is_____ fool-ish to men,_____ He must have seemed out of His mind. _____

e-ven His_____ fam-i-ly_____ said He was mad_____ and the priests said, "A de-mon's to blame;"

God in the form_ of this_____ an-gry young man could not have seemed per-fect-ly_____ sane.

GENTLE HANDS

By GERON DAV

GOT TO LET IT GO

By AMY GRANT, BROWN BANNISTER
SHANE KEISTER, MICHAEL W. SMITH
& GARY CHAPMAN

With a beat, not too fast

Additional Lyrics

2. You alone can see into the heart of me
Am I really givin' up tomorrow
Got to let it go
This is gonna hurt a little

Still it's right I know
Even tho I fear
Too much of me might show

I can't wait any longer for it
I've had enough
I'll give it up

3. Holdin' on too tight, Where do I lose sight
Where's the line that seems to bring frustration
Got to let it go
The best of dreams can turn to nightmares

When my heart takes hold
How long must I learn
This lesson's getting old

I've got to catch a clearer vision
I'm in your hand
You're in command

GOLIATH

By SCOTT WESLEY BROWN & PHIL NAIS

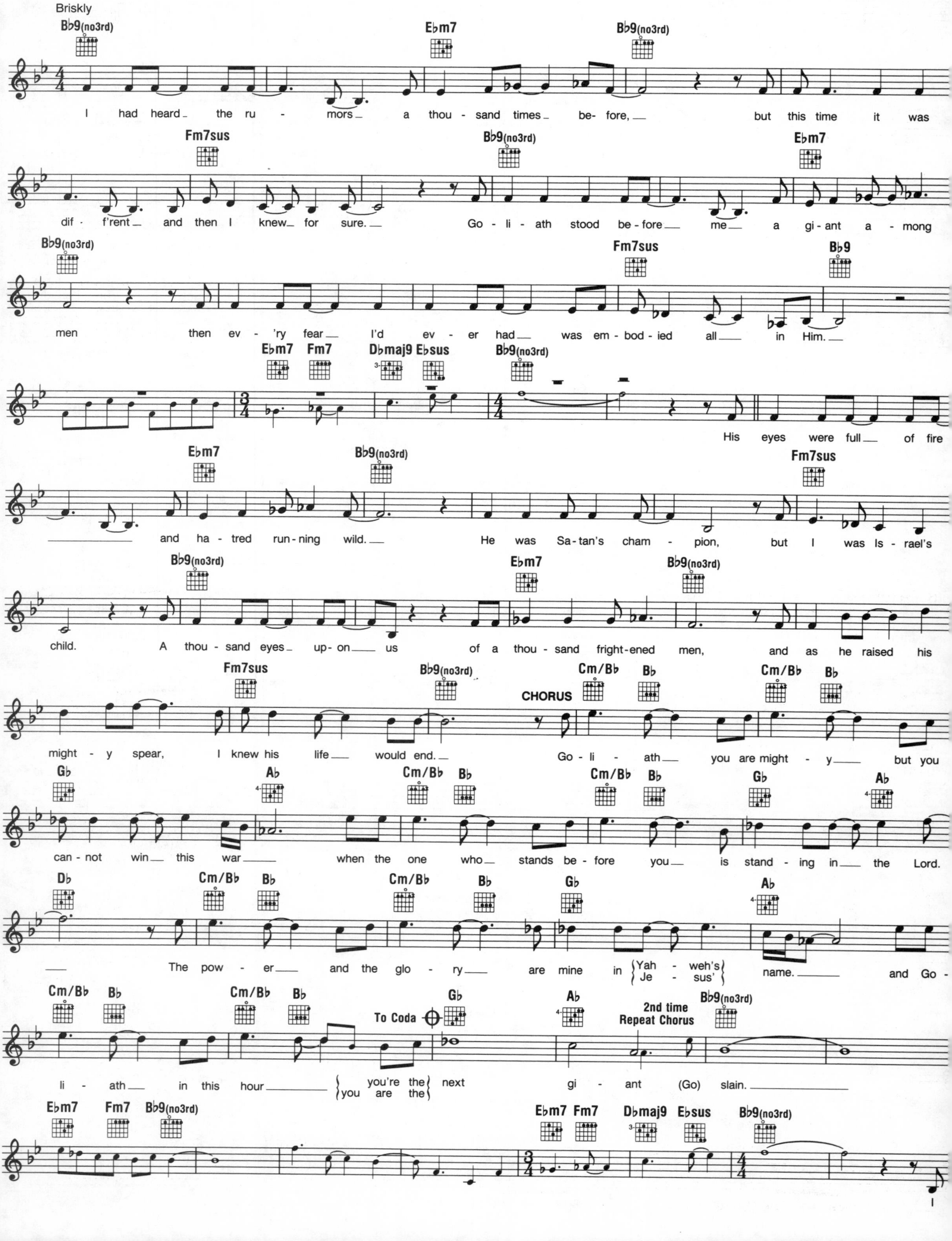

GREAT IS THE LORD

By MICHAEL W. SMITH
& DEBORAH D. SMITH

GRAVE ROBBER

Words and Music
BOB HARTM

GREATER IS HE THAT IS IN ME

By LANNY WOLFE

2. On the day of pentecost a rushing mighty wind
   blew into the upper room and baptized all of them.
   With a power greater than any earthly foe
   and I'm so glad I've got it too I'm gonna let the whole world know.

GOT TO TELL SOMEBODY

By DON FRANCI

5. Then Jesus touched my shoulder
   He told me not to grieve
   The trembling stopped when He looked
   and said "Only believe."
   Then He sent the crowds away except
   his closest men
   And they followed right behind us
   as we started off again.

6. But we were still a long ways down the road
   when I heard the sounds and cries
   Of the mourners and musicians
   as they strove to dramatize
   My grief they had no business with
   beneath their loud disguise
   And my wife just sat there silently
   and stared through empty eyes.

7. Then Jesus asked the mourners,
   "Why is it that you weep?
   She isn't dead as you suppose,
   the child is just asleep."
   It only took a moment for their
   wails to turn to jeers
   "Who does this man think he is?
   Get him out of here!"

3. I began to search the city
   and soon I saw the crowd
   They were pressing in to touch Him
   and they called his name out loud
   But with the strength of desperation
   I pushed them all aside
   I threw myself before Him
   and from my knees I cried
   BRIDGE #1

4. Well, He'd just begun to go with me
   when a face I saw with fear
   Came towards me with the news
   I knew I didn't want to hear
   And although I tried to steel myself
   I trembled when He said,
   "Why bother the teacher any more,
   your little girl is dead."

8. But with authority I've never heard
   in the lips of any man
   He spoke and every sound rolled out
   with the thunder of command
   And in the sudden silence
   they all hurried for the door
   Wondering what the reasons were
   they'd ever come there for.

9. Then He called His three disciples
   that were with Him on the way
   He led them and my wife and me
   to where our daughter lay
   He took her by the hand
   He told her, "Child, arise."
   And the words were barely spoken
   when she opened up her eyes.

10. BRIDGE #2

HE WAS THERE ALL THE TIME

By GARY S. PAXTON

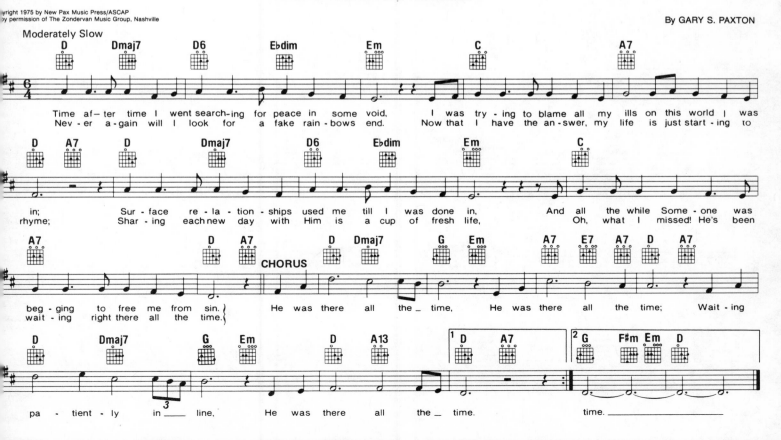

GOTTA HAVE THE REAL THING

By RICK R

HE SET MY LIFE TO MUSIC

By KYE FLEMING
& DENNIS W. MORGAN

HE HOLDS THE KEYS

By JON MO...

HE ROLLED AWAY THE STONE

Words and Music by TERRY SKINN
J. L. WALLACE & LONNIE LEDF

HE WILL CARRY YOU

982 Birdwing Music/Cherry Lane Music Publishing Co., Inc.

By SCOTT WESLEY BROWN

HE'LL SHINE HIS LIGHT ON YOU

By MICHELE PILLA
JAY GRUSKA & MARIE CA[...]

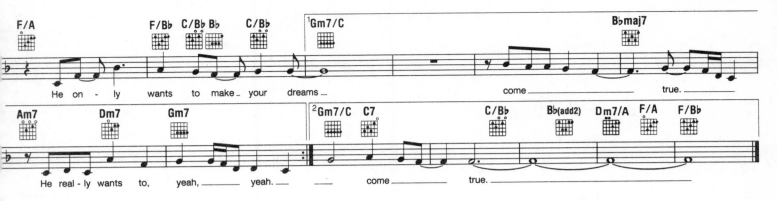

HEIRLOOMS

By AMY GRANT, BOB FARRELL
& BROWN BANNISTER

HE'S ALIVE

Words and Music
DON FRANCISCO

3. No one there but Mary and so I went down to let her in; John stood there beside me as she'd told us where she'd been. She said, "They moved Him in the night and none of us knows where; The stone's been rolled away and now His body isn't there!"

4. We both ran t'ward the garden, then John ran on ahead; We found the stone and the empty tomb just the way that Mary said. But the winding sheet they wrapped Him in was just an empty shell; And who or where they'd taken Him was more than I could tell.

5. Well, something strange had happened there, but just what I didn't know; John believed a miracle but I just turned to go. Circumstance and speculation couldn't lift me very high 'Cause I'd seen them crucify Him, then I saw Him die.

6. Back inside the house again the guilt and anguish came; Everything I'd promised Him just added to my shame. When at last it came to choices, I denied I knew His name; And even if He was alive, it wouldn't be the same.

7. But suddenly the air was filled with strange and sweet perfume; Light that came from everywhere drove shadows from the room. Jesus stood before me with His arms held open wide; And I fell down on my knees, and just clung to Him and cried.

8. He raised me to my feet, and as I looked into His eyes. Love was shining out from Him like sunlight in the ✛ To Coda

HEAVEN FELL LIKE RAIN
(When He Spoke)

Copyright 1986 by PRIME TIME MUSIC, (ASCAP), MASTERCRAFT MUSIC, (BMI), both divs. of Aaron Brown & Associates, Inc. and GRAND COALITION MUSIC, (BMI)., 1508 16th Ave. South; Nashville, TN 37212 USA   Used by Permission

Words and Music by MILTON CARROLL, BARBARA FAIRCHILD & MIKE SMITH

Slowly, with expression

HE'S ONLY A PRAYER AWAY

Words and Mus
HAL NEWMAN & SPOONER OLDI

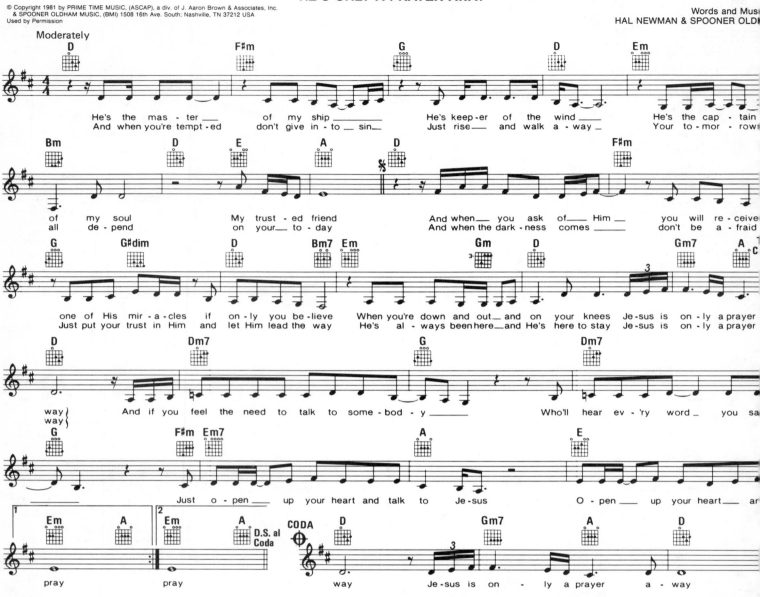

He's the mas-ter ___ of my ship ___ He's keep-er of the wind ___ He's the cap-tain
And when you're tempt-ed don't give in-to ___ sin ___ Just rise ___ and walk a-way ___ Your to-mor-rows

of my soul My trust-ed friend And when ___ you ask of ___ Him ___ you will re-ceive
all de-pend on your ___ to-day And when the dark-ness comes ___ don't be a-fraid

one of His mir-a-cles if on-ly you be-lieve When you're down and out and on your knees Je-sus is on-ly a prayer
Just put your trust in Him and let Him lead the way He's al-ways been here ___ and He's here to stay Je-sus is on-ly a prayer

way } And if you feel the need to talk to some-bod-y ___ Who'll hear ev-'ry word ___ you sa
way }

Just o-pen ___ up your heart and talk to Je-sus O-pen ___ up your heart ___ an

pray   pray

CODA

way   Je-sus is on - ly a prayer a - way

HOLINESS

By DON FRANCI

1. When God took his peo-ple to the prom-ised land, He gave them their free-dom and
2,3. (See additional lyrics)

gave a com-mand: ___ He said, "west of the Jor-dan you can have all you see but be

ware of their id-ols and be ho-ly to Me." Ho-li-ness, ___ Ho-li-ness: It's th

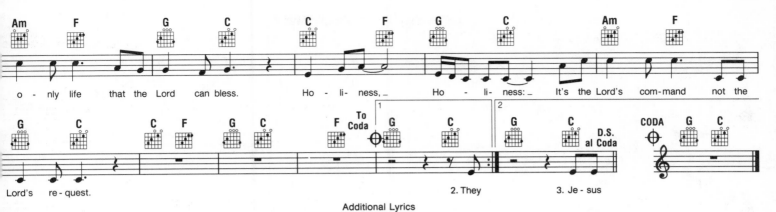

o - nly life that the Lord can bless. Ho - li - ness,_ Ho - li - ness: It's the Lord's com - mand not the

Lord's re - quest.

2. They   3. Je - sus

Additional Lyrics

2. They heard the commandment but did not obey.
They hardened their hearts and wandered away
from the goodness of God and the blessings He gave
the traditions of man and the yolk of a slave.

Holiness, holiness:
It's a life apart from the world's excess
for the people of God there remains a rest.
holiness, holiness.

3. Jesus is calling you come take my hand.
I'll lead you away from this wilderness land
to a place full of goodness as far as you see
but remember who brought you and be holy to Me.

Holiness, holiness:
It's not your food or drink it's not the way you dress.
holiness, holiness:
It's to hear the Lord and to answer yes.

Holiness, holiness:
It's the only life that the Lord can bless
For the people of God there remains a rest.
Holiness, holiness.

HOLD ON

Words and Music by
TONY BROWN & PAUL OVERSTREET

When you just don't fit in _ with ev - 'ry - one _ a - round _ you, _ the pres - ence of _ the dev -
feel that it's wrong, don't let _ them . per - suade _ you, _ there's al - ways _ some

- il _ keeps bring - in' you down. _ When you just don't feel right _ deep down in - side _
- bod - y who'll lead you a - stray. _ Don't be a fool _ and do what they're ask -

_ you, _ got to get a - hold of your - self, and _ turn it a - round. _
- in', Show _ them _ you're strong, _ and _ take them your way. _

turn it a - round, _
show them the way. _ } Hold on, and Je - sus will help _ you.

Hold on, _ and He'll be your friend. _ Keep on, _

ask and be giv - en. _ He'll be your strength _ if you hold on to Him.   Fine   When you

D.S. al Fine

THE HEART OF THE SEEKER

By JIM WE

1. Ev-'ry age ev-'ry new gen-e-ra-tion looks for truth they can claim as their own. Some get lost a
2. (See additional lyrics)

some just get cra-zy some give up when their hope is all gone {But the} {'cause the} heart of a seek-er dreams of the light.

longs for the sun-shine in the dead of night— and while an-oth-er bro-ther clos-es his eyes— and grows weak-er

God will give strength to The Heart— Of The Seek-er——

Additional Lyrics

2. In his heart the seeker is certain
He can ask someday he will receive
And he will find that the truth is a person
He can know if he'll only believe.

(CHORUS)

HELP ME LOVE MY BROTHER

Words and Mus
TANYA GOODMAN & MICHAEL SY

No man is an is-land, no man stands a-lone.— Lone-ly would the jour-ney be left
No man stands a-bove me and no man stands be-low.— The ground if lev-el— where y

trav-el on my own. Bro-thers— and sis-ters, let us join our hearts and hands. In love lift one an-oth-er
streams of mer-cy flow. We are cre-at-ed e-qual, in your spir-it we are one. Bro-thers and sis-ters in the

to the per-fect plan.} Lord Help Me Love My Bro-ther.— love him like he loves
sac-ri-fi-cial Son.}

me. If there be weak-ness in him, bind me to it by Your— love. Re-mind me we are per-fect-ed on

by grace from a-bove.— Lord, Help Me Love My Bro-ther.

HEAVENLY FATHER

By BILLY SPRAGUE & DAVID PARKS

HERE HE COMES WITH MY HEART

By LESLIE PHILL[

HERE I AM

Words and Music by CHRIS EATON,
RUSS TAFF & TORI TAFF

HIS GRACE IS GREATER

By GREG NELSON, PHILL McHU
STEVE GREEN & LARI GO

His Grace _____ Is Great-er than our fail - ures ___ His peace _____ runs deep-er than ou

(see additional lyrics)

fears _____ If we go to Him for mer - cy our hearts can rest as - sured His

love _____ will keep us through our tears _____ He'll hand _____ Though

count - less souls have come to Him so des - p'rate and lost with faith no great - er than a tin - y

seed Each one has found a won - drous truth be - neath His sim - ple cross His

Grace _____ Is Great - er than our need _____ No tears. _____

Additional Lyrics

2. He'll give us strength to simply trust Him
Through times we may not understand
We will gain a sweet assurance
No passing doubt can dim
Our lives are safely in His hand.

3. No height or depth in all creation
Can reach beyond His love for me
And His power has raised my spirit
The work forever done
With grace far greater than my need.

HOLY, HOLY

By MICHAEL W. SMITH, DEBORAH D. SMI
BROWN BANNISTER & DEBBIE BANNIST

Ho - ly, Ho - ly. Ho - ly, Ho - ly. Ho - ly is the Lord

God Al - might - y. Ho - ly, Ho - ly. Ho - ly, Ho - ly. Ho - ly is the Lord

HOLLOW EYES

Words and Music
BOB HARTMAN

Moderately, in "4"

An - oth - er day___ in Ni - ger - i - a___ the chil - dren beg for___ bread, ___ the
crowd - ed sheds the chil - dren lay their heads___ to es - cape the Hai - tian___ heat. ___ The

crops have failed, ___ the well ran dry___ when they lost the wa - ter - shed. ___ A ba - by dies, ___ its
hun - ger pains drive them to the street___ won - d'ring if to - day they'll eat. ___ Some find food in the

moth - er cries, ___ the chil - dren gath - er ___ 'round. ___ They're won - der - ing ___ what the
re - fuse heap, ___ oth - ers find ___ di - sease, ___ some find it hard - er

day will bring, ___ will they be the next one found?___ Do you dare___ to gaze in - to the
just to live___ when they can die with ease, ___ His

Hol - low Eyes, ___ Hol - low Eyes?___ Are they star - ing holes in you___ with their
Is He star - ing back at you with His Hol - low Eyes, ___

Hol - low Eyes, ___ Hol - low Eyes?___ In the The least of these___ is hu -

- gry. The least of these___ is sick. The least of these___needs cloth - ing. The least of these___needs drink.

The least of these___knows sor - row. The least of these___knows grief. ___ The least of these___ has

D.S. al Coda

suf - fered pain, and Je - sus is___ His name. ___

CODA

Hol - low Eyes, ___ Hol - low Eyes?

HOLY GROUND

By GERON DAVIS

Worshipfully

HOLY IS HIS NAME

By JOHN MICHAEL TALBOT

With conviction

My soul ___ pro-claims the great - ness of the Lord _____ and my spir - it ex-
mer - cy in ev - 'ry gen - er - a - tion, He has re - vealed ____ His

alts in God my Sav - ior. For He has looked ____ with mer - cy on my low - li - ness and my
pow - er and His glo - ry. He has cast down ____ the might - y in their ar - ro-gance, and has

name will be for - ev - er ex - alt - ed. For the might - y God ___ has done great things for me
lift - ed up the meek and the low - ly. He has come to help ___ His ser - vant Is - ra - el

and His mer - cy ____ will reach from age to age. ____ And ___ Ho - ly,
He ___ re - mem - bers His prom - ise to our Fa - thers.

Ho - ly, Ho - ly Is His ___ Name. _____ He has And ___ Ho -

ly, Ho - ly, Ho - ly Is His __ Name. _____ And ___

HOSANNA

By MICHAEL W. SMITH
& DEBORAH D. SMITH

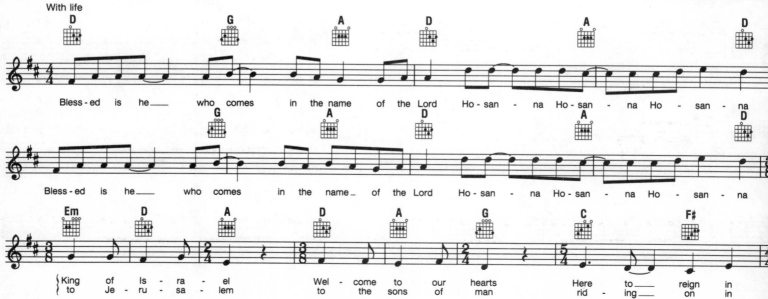

With life

Bless - ed is he ___ who comes in the name of the Lord Ho - san - na Ho - san - na Ho - san - na

Bless - ed is he ___ who comes in the name of the Lord Ho - san - na Ho - san - na Ho - san - na

King of Is - ra - el Wel - come to our hearts Here to ___ reign in
to Je - ru - sa - lem to the sons of man rid - ing ___ on in

Home Where I Belong

By PAT TER

HOW CAN THEY LIVE WITHOUT JESUS?

By KEITH GRE

HOW COULD I EVER SAY NO

By JAMIE OWENS-COLL

With movement

A whis-per in the wind as it blows a-cross my heart, and I hear You call my name, so get-tle an
Lord, You asked for much but You've giv-en so much more. You e-ven give the strength I need to

low.
bey You. You ask for ev-'ry-thing I have ev-er count-ed dear, And, a
You gave your life for me, so I give my life to You, But if

first my trem-bled hands are a-fraid to let go. You. But Af-ter all You've
give 'til time runs out, I can nev-er re-pay

giv-en and af-ter all You've done. Oh, af-ter all it cost You to pay for m

soul. How Could I Ev-er Say No.

My No. Oh, No? Lord, How Could

Ev-er Say No? Lord, How Could

HOW MAJESTIC IS YOUR NAME

By MICHAEL W. SMIT

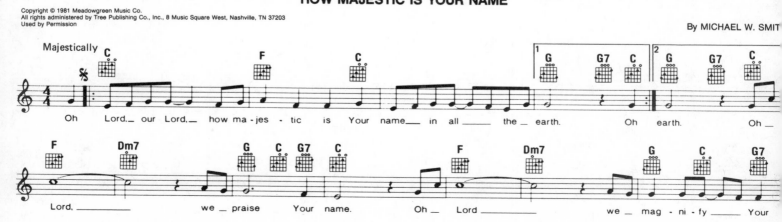

Majestically

Oh Lord, our Lord, how ma-jes-tic is Your name in all the earth. Oh earth. Oh

Lord, we praise Your name. Oh Lord we mag-ni-fy Your

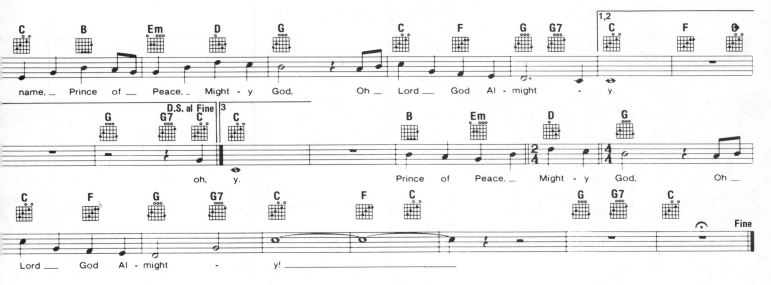

name,___ Prince of ___ Peace,___ Might-y God, Oh ___ Lord ___ God Al-might ___ -y.

oh, y. Prince of Peace.___ Might-y God, Oh ___

Lord ___ God Al-might ___ -y!

HYMN

By RANDY STONEHILL

Flowing

In this land of the walk-ing wound-ed, In this des-ert of count-less sor-rows,
In my heart I have made this pro-mise and with this song I de-clare my choice.

I will cling to His hand to-day and fear not for to-mor-___ row.
I will walk where the shep-herd leads and head no oth-er voice. ___ In the chill of my

dark-est hour ___ I am saved from my deep des-pair, ___ for the Fath-er who loves His child-ren

hears my trust-ing prayer. ___ Oo ___

In my soul there is
In the end we are

one light shin-ing from the flame of my true be-lief, and its em-bers can-not be quenched or
not for-got-ten and our jour-ney is not in vain, for the mas-ter who brought us here will

robbed by an-y thief. ___ lead us home, ___ lead us home a-gain.

HOSANNA, GLORIA

Words and Music
BOB FARRELL & DAVE ROBB

I AM HE

By TERRY TALBOT

I AM SURE

By MICHAEL W. SM
& MIKE HUDS

I CAN SEE

Words by GLORIA GAITHER with DAVID MEECE
Music by DAVID MEECE

I AM LOVED

Words by WILLIAM J. GAITHER & GLORIA GAITHER
Music by WILLIAM J. GAITHER

I LOVE YOU

By AMY GRANT
& MICHAEL W. SMITH

I DEDICATE ALL MY LOVE TO YOU

By TERI DeSARIO PURSE & BILL PU

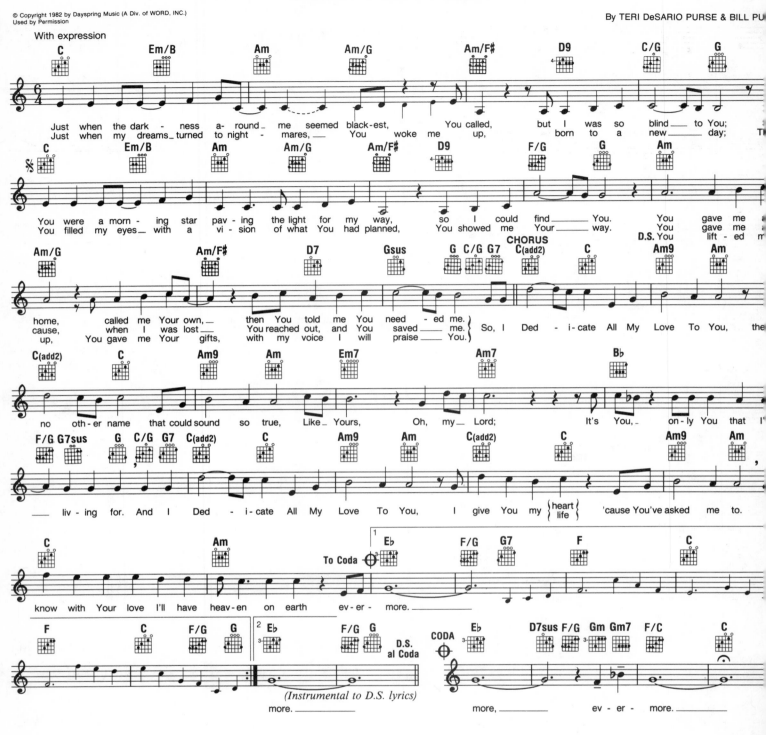

(Instrumental to D.S. lyrics)

I WANT TO MAKE A DIFFERENCE

By MICHELE PILLAR & JOHN L

I WANT TO KNOW CHRIST

Words by MICHAEL HUDS
Music by GARY DRISK

Additional Lyrics

2. I know that my path is the way of the cross
But I count what I gain and forget what I've lost
In pain there is joy — in death there is life
Dear God, hear my cry — I Want To Know Christ

I WANT TO BE A CLONE

By STEVE TAYLOR

83 C.A. Music/Birdwing Music/Cherry Lane Music Publishing Co., Inc.

With driving energy

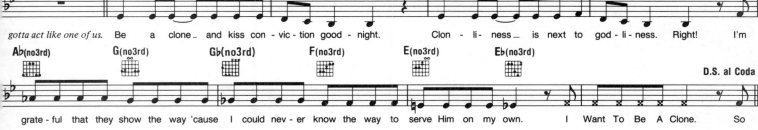

I'd gone thru so much oth-er stuff that walk-ing down the aisle was tough. But now I know it's not e-nough. I
told me that I'd fall a-way, un-less I fol-lowed what they say. Who needs the Bi-ble an-y-way. I
now I see the whole de-sign, My church is an as-sem-bly line. The parts are there, I'm feel-ing fine. I

Want To Be A Clone. I asked the Lord in-to my heart they said that was the way to start. But now you've got to play the part. I
Want To Be A Clone. Their lan-guage it was new to me, but Chris-tian-ese got thru to me. Now I can speak it flu-ent-ly. I
Want To Be A Clone. I've learned e-nough to stay a-float, but not so much I rock the boat. I'm glad they shoved it down my throat. I

Want To Be A Clone.
Want To Be A Clone. Be a clone and kiss con-vic-tion good-night. Clon-li-ness is next to god-li-ness. Right! I'm

grate-ful that they show the way, 'cause I could nev-er know the way to serve Him on my own. I Want To Be A Clone. They

Want To Be A Clone. Send in the clones. *Spoken: Ah, I kinda*

wanted to tell my friends and people about it, ya know? What? You're still a babe. You have to grow. Give it twenty years or so, 'cause if you wanna be one of His,

gotta act like one of us. Be a clone and kiss con-vic-tion good-night. Clon-li-ness is next to god-li-ness. Right! I'm

grate-ful that they show the way 'cause I could nev-er know the way to serve Him on my own. I Want To Be A Clone. So

D.S. al Coda

CODA

Want To Be A Clone.

Spoken: Everybody must get cloned!

I JUST FEEL LIKE SOMETHING GOOD IS ABOUT TO HAPPEN

Words and Music
WILLIAM J. GAIT..

3. Yes, I've noticed all the bad news in the paper, And it seems like things are bleaker every day;
But for this child of God it makes no difference, Because it's bound to get better either way.
I've never been more thrilled about tomorrow, Sunshines always bursting thru the skies of gray;

I'M GONNA FLY

By AMY GR..

I HAVE DECIDED

By MICHAEL CA[...]

With conviction

I Have De - cid - ed I'm gon-na live__ like a be - liev - er. Turn my back__ on the de-ceiv - er, Gon-na

live what I__ be - lieve; I Have De - cid - ed be - ing good__ is just a fa - ble I just can

__ 'cause I'm not a - ble, Gon - na leave it to__ the Lord.

There's a wealth of things__ that I pro-fessed, I
So for-get the game__ of be - ing good__ and

said that I__ be - lieved. But deep in-side__ I nev - er changed, I__ guess I'd been de-ceived;__ A
your self - right - eous pain, Cause the on - ly good__ in - side your heart__ is the good that Je - sus brings;__ When th

voice in - side__ kept tell - ing me__ that I'd change by__ and by, But the Spir - it made__ it clear to me__ that __
world be - gins__ to see you change, don't ex - pect them to ap - plaud, Keep your eyes on Him__ and tell your self:__ I've b

1. kind of life's a lie. I Have De - gun the work__ of God. I Have De - cid - ed I'm gon-na live
2. like a be - liev - er. Turn my back__ on the de-ceiv - er. Gon-na live what I__ be - lieve; I Have De -

cid - ed be - ing good__ is just a fa - ble I just can't__ 'cause I'm not a - ble, Gon - na leave it to__ the Lord.

IN HIS NAME

By MARK GERSMEH[...]

Slowly with purpose

The eyes of the world_____ are cry - ing, sor - row is an old fa - mi - liar
He is the vine,_____ we are branch - es, the pow - er that we have_____ comes from

I KNOW

Words and Mus
MICHAEL W. SMITH & WAYNE KIRKPAT

I LOVE A LONELY DAY

By GARY CHAPMAN & MICHAEL W. SM

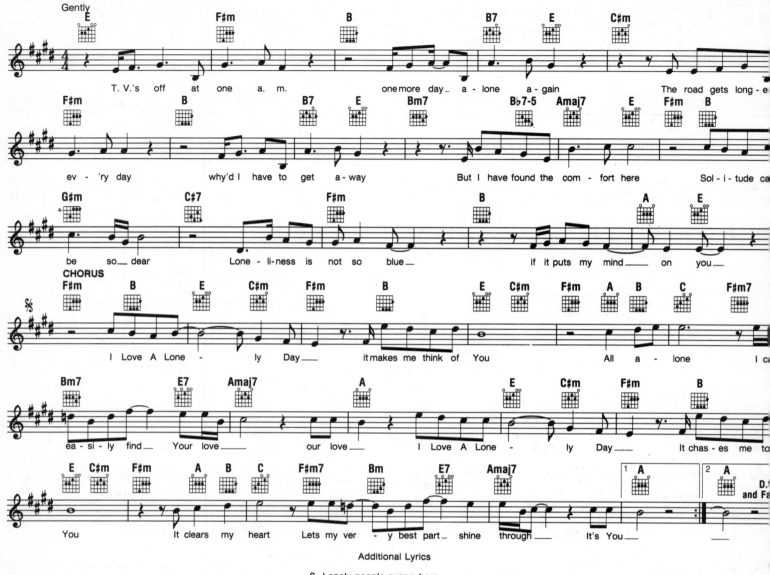

Additional Lyrics

2. Lonely people everywhere
   Lucky lonely ones who care
   You've got all you need and more
   Someone to be lonely for
   Someone cries for you to hear
   Take your heart and wipe their tear
   Give them someone they can miss
   Give them love and sing them this

   Chorus

I WALKED TODAY

By GREG NELSON & GLORIA GAITH

F   C/G   F/G   G To Coda ⊕   ① C   ② C

in   Yes, I walked with Je-sus there   to- day.   I saw the day.   I saw the day.

BRIDGE
Dm   G   C/G   Ab+   Am   Am/G   F

Where the least of all   find no place   to turn   and they fall   with-

Bb   Gsus   G   C   D.S. al Coda   CODA C

out   a name.   Je - sus   day.

Additional Lyrics

2. I saw the Lord behind the eyes
Of the broken men
And I felt His wounded hand
Reach out
And as the careless traffic sped
Along the other side
I saw Jesus walk the streets today

Bridge: Where the least of all
Find no place to turn
And they fall without a name —

3. Jesus walks with these —
The hungry and the lost
Off'ring water from a cup and bread
The bread of life, the living stream;
Where teaming millions cross
To find that God, God Himself, walks there

IF ONLY

By JACK FOWLER & KATHY TROCCOLI

Slowly
D   A/C#   D   A/C#   Em7   Em7/A   A7   D

Mem - or - ies you made with me still fill my mind When you died I
Man - y tears have filled the years and as I grew There were times that

Bm   A/C#   Em7   G   A   F#/A#   Bm   E7

ques-tioned why a thou-sand times It hurt to have to say good-bye
I would find me mis-sing you And e - ven though I'm old - er now

Bm   Bm/A   E7   G   A7   D

With-out a chance to say a lit-tle more And If On - ly you could
I nev - er have out - grown my need for you

Gm   D   Gm   Bm   G To Coda ⊕

hold me now and If on - ly you could know some - how All the love I'd long to show Oh

Em   Gm   ① D A/C# D A/C# Em7 Em7/A A7   ② D   Gm   D.S. al Coda

dad - dy If On - ly you could know know And If

CODA Em7   Gm   D A/C# D A/C# Em7   D

dad - dy dad - dy Some - how I think you know

I'D RATHER BELIEVE IN YOU

Words by STORMIE OMART...
Music by MICHAEL OMART...

I'VE HEARD THE THUNDER

By LEON PATILLO

I'VE JUST SEEN JESUS

Words by GLORIA GAIT
Music by WILLIAM J. GAITHER & DANNY DAN

In A Little While

By AMY GRANT, GARY CHAPM
SHANE KEISTER & BROWN BANNIS

IN THE PROMISED LAND

Copyright 1985 by Patch Music Ltd.
By Permission

By CHRIS EATON

I'M UP

By MICHAEL W. S[mith]
& MIKE HUD[son]

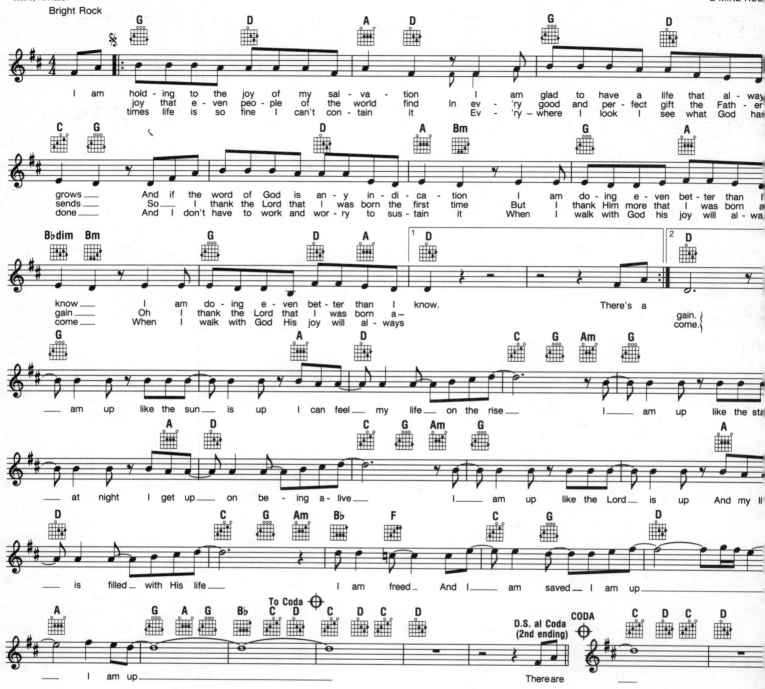

IN THE NAME OF THE LORD

By PHILL McHUGH, GLORIA GAITH[er]
& SANDI PATTI HELVER[ing]

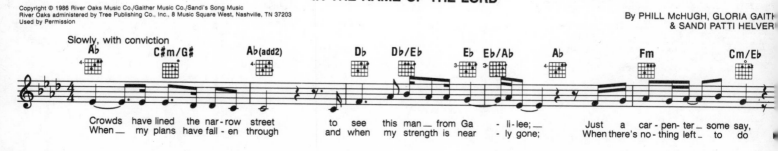

IT WAS ENOUGH

By LARRY BRY/

Additional Lyrics

D.S. 3. It Was Enough the life that I gave,
It Was Enough that I conquered the grave.
It Was Enough to pay for your sin,
It Was Enough that you died for me.

D.S. (2nd time) 4. It Was Enough the blood that I shed,
It Was Enough that I rose from the dead.
It Was Enough nothing more I could do,
It Was Enough that I died for you.

IT'S NOT A SONG

By GARY CHAPMAN
& ROBBIE BUCHANAN

Moderate funk

IT IS GOOD

Words and Mus
JIM WEBER & NILES BO

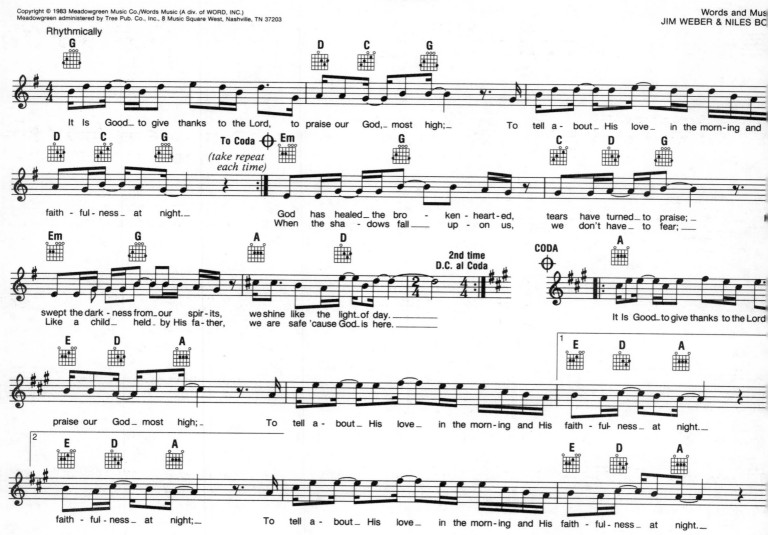

JESUS IS LORD

By DONNA DOUGL

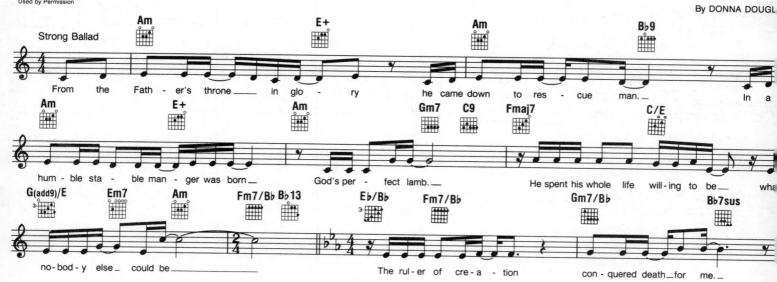

IT'S JUST THE FIRST FAREWELL

By TONY ELENBURG

Additional lyrics

This bread it is my body, This wine it is my blood
When night falls I will leave here
Just remember what I've said and done.

JEHOVAH

By GEOFF THURMAN

JERICHO

By MICHAEL W. SM...
PAUL SMITH & MIKE HUD...

JESUS CALL YOUR LAMBS

By TERI DeSARIO PURSE

JESUS IN YOUR HEART

By MARK BALD

JESUS, LORD TO ME

By GREG NELSON & GARY McSPADDEN

JESUS NEVER FAILS

Words and Music
GARY DRISK

1. So man-y souls have test-ed him thru-out the course of time so man-y still reach out to him
2. (See additional lyrics)

bro-ken hearts and minds and eve-ry one of them will sing with no ex-cep-tion that they find

Je - sus nev - er fails ev - en in the days of old He brought his peo - ple through

then he came to show his love and died for me and you and he rose a - gain to prove that ev - 'ry s

- y had been true Je - sus Nev - er Fails Je - sus Ne - ver Fails

CHORUS

Je - sus Ne - ver Fails you might as well get thee be - hind me sa - tan

you can - not pre - vail be - cause Je - sus Ne - ver Fails.

Fine   D.C. al

Additional Lyrics

2. Sometimes this world brings troubles we find so hard to bear
We know we couldn't make it without Jesus being there
It's so encouraging to know however deep we're in despair
Jesus never fails

So what can I do to prove this to you but tell me how can you deny
There are no untold facts no mysteries it's all so ''cut and dry''
On the witness stand of life, I'll be the first to testify
Chorus:

KEEPIN' MY EYES ON YOU

By TWILA PA

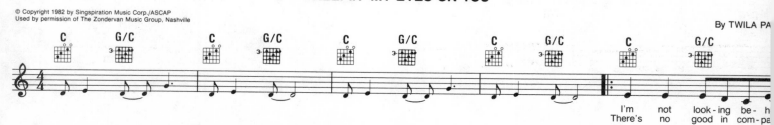

I'm not look - ing be -
There's no good in com - pa -

JUDE DOXOLOGY

By MICHAEL W. SM

KEEP THE FLAME BURNING

By DAVID BINION
& CAROL (CONNIE) NELSON

The King Of Who I Am

Words and Music
TANYA GOODMAN & MICHAEL SYK

Slowly and Serenely

My days are filled with laugh-ter,_ my heart has known your peace._ I've tra-veled far,_ still there is far to

go._ 'Cause in my heart there is a long - ing_ to look up-on_ Your face._

Where You are is where I want to be._ You_ are my King; You are the Lamb;_

Li-on of Ju-dah, seed of A-bra-ham,_ the Ho-ly One,_ God's_ on-ly Son. Y

To Coda

are_ The King_ Of Who I_ Am.

road I've tra-veled down_ You have walked be-fore me,_ made the light_ to shine_ out of dark - ness. I a

D.S. al C

look-ing for the day_ when I_ bow be-fore_ You, lay my crown_ at Your feet._ You

CODA

Am._ Ooh_

KINGDOM OF LOVE

By SCOTT WESLEY BRO
BILLY SMILEY & MARK GERSM

Moderately
VERSE

Take a look a-round_ what do you see
Time is run-ning out_ but it's not too late

There are so
There's a worl

KNOWN BY THE SCARS

By MICHAEL C

LET THE WHOLE WORLD SING

By ED DeGARMO,
DANA KEY & BOB FARRELL

LAMB OF GLORY

Words and Musi
PHILL McHUGH & GREG NEL

LAZARUS COME FORTH

By CARMAN LICCIARDELLO

Moderately

*Spoken) I am the Resurrection and
the Life, He who believeth*   *in Me, though he were
dead, yet shall he live.*

1. A cer - tain man__ had died___ in the town of Beth - a - ny___ and
(2.) died he went__ to where ___ the saints of God did stay in the

Laz - ar - us___ was his name.   The Bib - le says__ he was___ a
hold - ing place they lived be - yond the tomb.   There he saw__ E - li - jah, Mos - es,

man that Je - sus loved   and his sis - ters thought it was a shame.   Mar - y and Mar - tha longed for Je -
Sam - u - el, e - ven Ruth, and all the oth - ers jammed up in a room.   He turned a - round and saw ol' Gid - eon

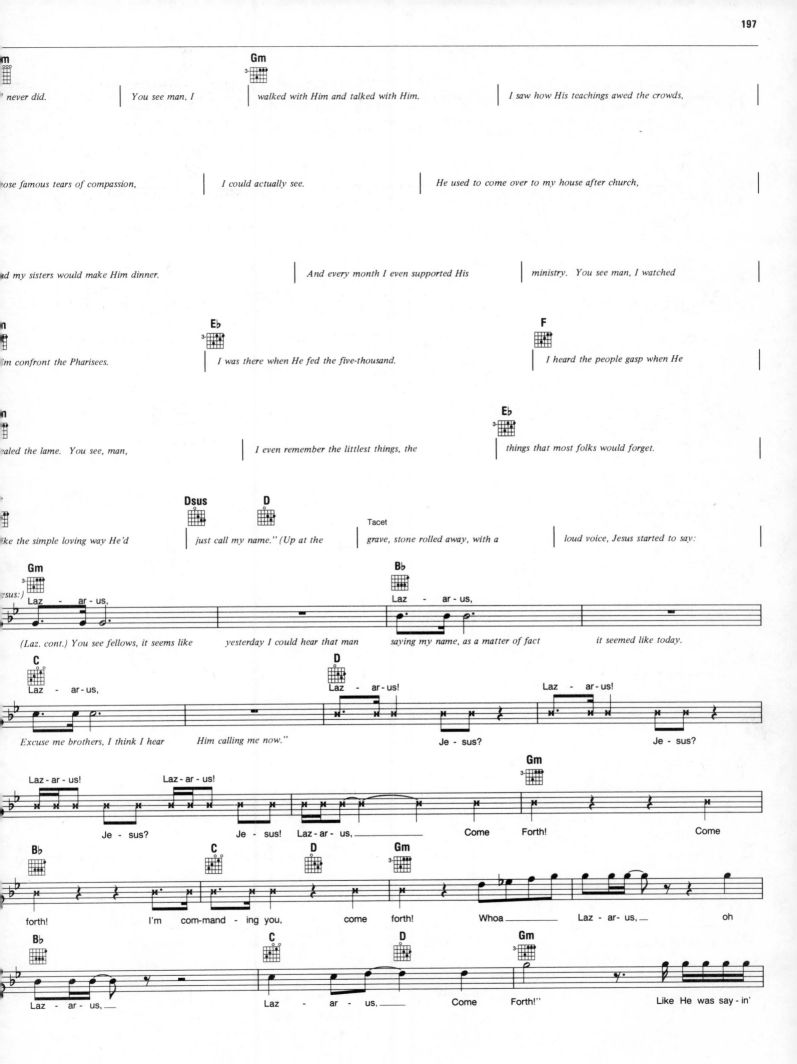

LET THERE BE PRAISE

By MELODIE TUNNEY & DICK TUNN[EY]

With expression

CHORUS

Let There Be Praise, let there be joy in our hearts. Sing to the Lord give Him the

Glo- ry Let There Be Praise, Let there be joy in our hearts

For- ev- er more let His love fill the air and Let There Be Praise.

VERSE

1. He in- hab- its the praise of His peo- ple and dwells deep with- in Th[e]
2. (See additional lyrics)

peace that He gives none can e- qual His love it knows no end. So lift your voi- ces

with glad- ness. Sing pro- claim through all the Earth that Je- sus Christ is King.

Additional Lyrics

2. When the Spirit of God is with us
   We will overcome
   In our weakness, His strength will defend us
   When His praise is on our tongue
   So lift your voices
   With gladness sing
   Proclaim through all the Earth
   That Jesus Christ is King

LAMB OF GOD

Words and Music by
TWILA PARIS

With movement

Your on-ly Son no sin to hide, But You have sent Him from Your side To walk up-on this guilt-y

sod and to be-come the Lamb Of God. Your gift of love they cru-ci-fied, They laughed and

scorned Him as He died, the hum-ble King they named a fraud And sac-ri-ficed the Lamb Of God. Oh, Lamb Of

God, sweet Lamb Of God, I love the ho-ly Lamb Of God. Oh, wash me in His pre-cious

blood, My Je-sus Christ, the Lamb Of God. I was so

lost, I should have died, But You have brought me to Your side to be led by Your staff and rod, And to be

called a Lamb Of God. Oh, Lamb Of God, sweet Lamb Of God, I love the ho-ly Lamb Of

God; Oh, wash me in His pre-cious blood till I am just a Lamb Of God. Oh, wash me

in His pre-cious blood, My Je-sus Christ, the Lamb Of God.

LAMBS IN THE VALLEY

Words by CHARLENE CA[...]
Music by WILLIAM RICHARD[...]

Slowly, with dignity

Lord, take our hands. We are Lambs In The Val - ley. We know You'll al - ways b[...]
Lord, take our hands. We are Lambs In The Val - ley. No man walks through it

there. And Lord, when we fall, help us stand in the val - ley. With cour - age each
lone. And Lord, though our souls some-times cry out in an - guish, we know that we

cross we will bear. Then, by the {still, still wa - ters, we will drink, we w[...]
soon will be home. By the {

heed the com - mand to be the sons and daugh - ters of the

One who is the great I Am._____ Lord, take our hands. We are Lambs In The Val - ley.

LOVE OF ANOTHER KIND

By RICHARD MULLINS, WAYNE KIRKPATR[...]
AMY GRANT & GARY CHAP[...]

Fast, with excitement

They say__ love__ is cruel, They say__ love__ is ra - ther fra - gile,
They say__ love__ brings hurt, I say__ love__ brings heal - ing,
They say__ love__ won't last, I say__ love__ is nev - er - end - ing,

but I've__ found__ in__ you it's} a Love Of An - oth - er__ Kind,_____ Love Of An - oth - er Ki[...]
un - der - stand - ing first
'cause in__ you__ I have

The love I know_____ is a love so few dis - cov - er, they need to kno[...]

Je - sus' love__ is__ like__ no oth - er.__ Love Of An - oth - er Ki[...]

D.C. al Coda

CODA

LET THE WIND BLOW

By DAVID C. MARTIN & PHIL N

Wind _____ Blow, _____ up- on _____ the Sol- id Rock _____ of God _____ I _____ stand. _____

_____ Let The Wind ____ Blow, _____ Let The Wind ____ Blow. ____ Let the rain _____ fall _____ down. from the sky

_____ give all ____ the ____ hurt _____

- ty pow- er ____ be

optional ending

Repeat ad lib and Fade

____ a - bove, let the tem - pest roar ____ till it's had ____ e - nough. Let the world ____

- it can, let the ev - il one de - vise ____ his ____ plans. Let its might-

- un - leashed, let the doubt - ers fall up - on ____ their ____ knees. Let the rain ____

LOOK HOW FAR YOU'VE COME

By JAMIE OWENS-COLLINS
& CHRIS CHRISTIAN

So you've lost your will to win. ____ Seems you're down to your last ____ friend; And the weight of the world ____ keeps ____

failed at plans you've laid, ____ Don't for - get the steps you've ____ made. He has brought you this far, ____ He ____ can

try - ing to pull ____ you in. ____ Don't give up, Don't give in, Give it all ____ to Him, 'cause He cares so much more than you

take you the rest of the ____ way. ____

know. ____ When it seems who you real - ly ____ want to ____ be is some - one you'll nev - er be - come, ____ Just

Look How Far ____ You've Come. ____ Though you've ____ Come. I know it's not al - ways ea - sy But don't throw it all a -

way, ____ You've come too far to turn back now. You're head - in' home, ____ and you're not a - lone. Don't give

look how far, ____ Don't for - get how ____ far, ____ Just Look How Far ____ You've Come. ____

LET THEM GO

Words and Music by TANYA GOODM
JEFF ROSS & MICHAEL SYF

A LITTLE GOOD NEWS

Words and Music by CHARLIE BLACK,
RORY BOURKE & TOMMY ROCCO

LIFT HIM UP

Words and Mu[...]
DON JA[...]

LOVE EVERYBODY IN THE WORLD

Words and Music by
TANYA GOODMAN & MICHAEL SYKES

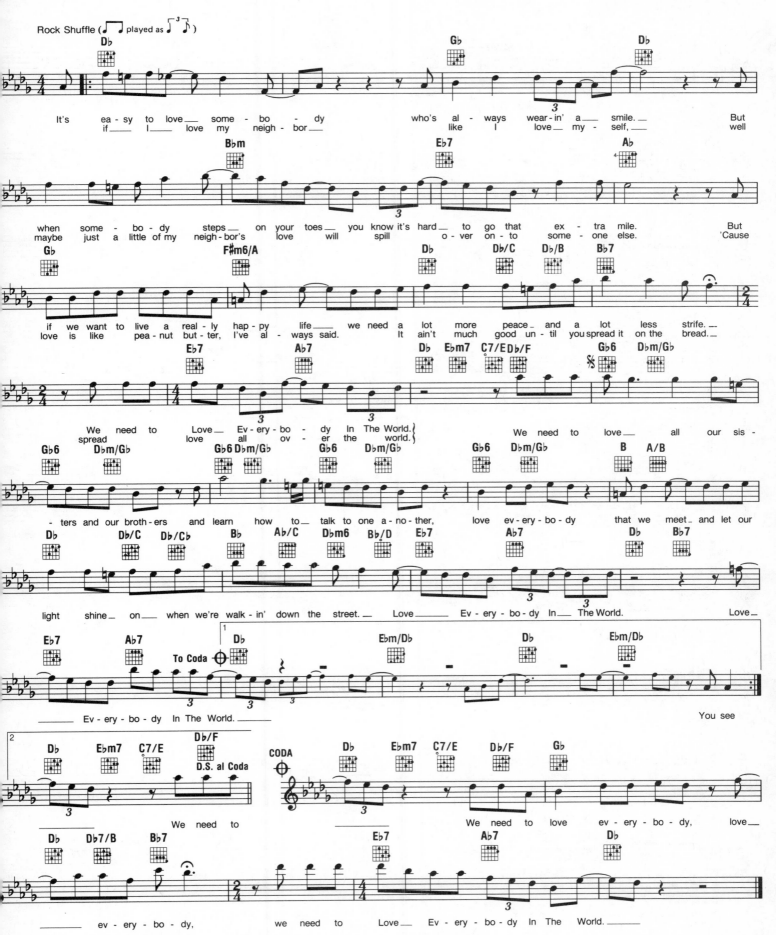

LIVING IN LAODICEA

By STEVE CA...

LOVE NEVER FAILS

Words and Music by
TANYA GOODMAN & MICHAEL SYKES

Look Who Loves You Now

By STEVE STO...

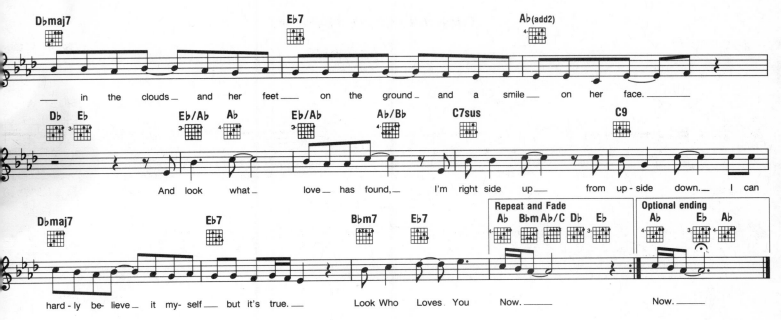

Dbmaj7 Eb7 Ab(add2)
... in the clouds and her feet on the ground and a smile on her face.

Db Eb Eb/Ab Ab Eb/Ab Ab/Bb C7sus C9
And look what love has found, I'm right side up from up-side down. I can

Dbmaj7 Eb7 Bbm7 Eb7
Repeat and Fade: Ab Bbm Ab/C Db Eb
Optional ending: Ab Eb Ab
hard-ly be-lieve it my-self but it's true. Look Who Loves You Now. Now.

LOVE FOUND A WAY

By GREG NELSON & PHILL McHUGH

With meaning

D G/D A/D D D G/D
An an-gel stood, with flam-ing sword, at E-den's dark-ened gate;
na-tion grew to bring one man a vir-gin would con-ceive;
The fright-ened fam-'ly faced a world now
A man who died, then rose with life for

A/D D F Bbmaj7 A7sus A D
filled with Sa-tan's hate. These fal-len chil-dren God so loved were lost in fear a-lone, now
all who will be-lieve. For ev-'ry child of A-dam's race who longs to leave des-pair, the

F Bbmaj7 G/A A D/F# G A A/G F#m7 G
love would stand no cost to bring them home. Love Found A Way, Love Found A Way, and our
road that leads us home thro' love is there. Love Found A

D D/F# E E/G# A7sus D D/F# G F#7sus F#7 Bm Bb D/A G/A
hearts can hold the price love chose to pay. All hope was gone 'til Eas-ter's dawn; We are free be-cause Love Found A
To Coda

1. Bb Gm D F Bbmaj7
Way.
2. D D/F#
D.S. al Coda
One Way. Love Found A

CODA D D/F# G F#7sus F#7
Way. Love Found A

Bm Bb D/A G/A Bb C D C F Bb D
Way; We are free be-cause Love Found A Way.

LOOKIN' OUT FOR NUMBER ONE

By WAYNE WATSON

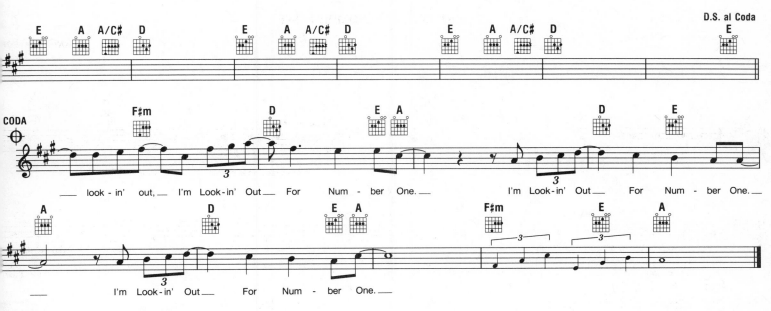

LORD OF THE DANCE

Words and Music by
SYDNEY CARTER

Additional Lyrics

3. I danced on the Sabbath and I cured the lame,
The holy people, they said it was a shame,
They whipped and they stripped and they hung me high,
And they left me there on a cross to die.
Chorus

4. I danced on a Friday when the sky turned black,
It's hard to dance with the devil on your back,
They buried my body and they thought I'd gone,
But I am the dance and I still go on.
Chorus

5. They cut me down and I leap up high.
I am the life that'll never, never die,
I'll live in you if you'll live in me,
I am the Lord of the Dance, said He.
Chorus

LORD OF GLORY

By MARK GERSME

LOSING GAME

By DALLAS HOLM

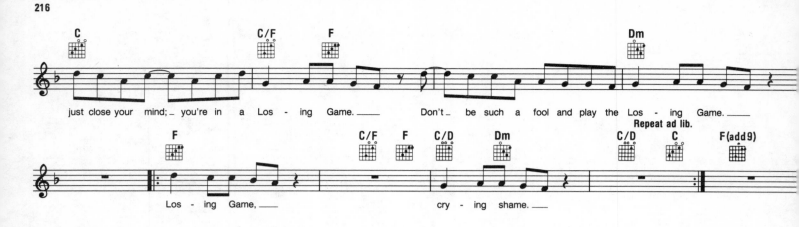

LOVE IN ANY LANGUAGE

By JON MOHR & JOHN MAY

straight from the heart,____ pulls us all____ to-geth - er,____ nev - er a- part;____ And

once we learn____ to speak it____ all the world____ will hear____ Love In A - ny Lan - guage____

flu-ent-ly spok - en____ here. Though the rhe - tor - ic of gov - ern-ments may keep us worlds____ a-part,

____ There's no mis - in-ter - pret - ing the lan - guage of the heart.____

Love In An - y Lan - guage, straight from____ the heart,____ pulls us all____ to-geth - er,

nev - er a- part;____ And once we learn____ to speak it_____ all the world____ will hear____

Love In An - y Lan - guage flu-ent-ly spo - ken____ here. here. Love In An - y Lan -

- guage flu-ent-ly spo - ken____ here. Love In An - y Lan - guage flu - ent - ly

spo - ken here.____ Love In An - y Lan - guage spo - ken_____ here.____

LOVE CALLING

By LEON PATILLO

MAKE MY HEART YOUR HOME

By PAUL SMITH
& KEITH THOMAS

LOVE THEM WHILE WE CAN

By MARK GERSM

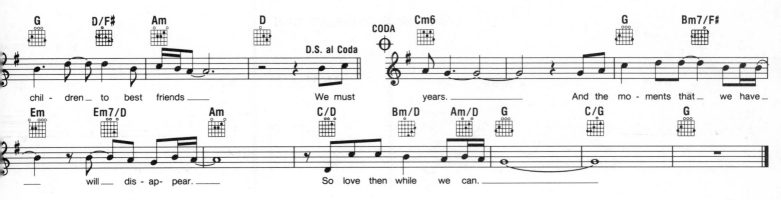

MAKER OF MY HEART

By ROBERT J. KAUFLIN

MAN IN THE MIDDLE

Words and Music
MICKEY CATE

Moderately, in "2"

I nev-er worked one hon-est day, took my liv-in' from oth-er folk's pay;
Ev-'ry man is a thief in some light, steal-ing from God now you know that ain't right;

I knew one day they'd catch up with me___ now they've nailed me up___ for the world to see.
Tak-ing His time, tak-ing His name,___ tak-ing His Word,___ tak-ing it all in vain.

Now there's a man___ on the oth-er side of this hill, and just like me___ he was
Ev-'ry thief has a price on his head,___ but Je-sus paid it all with the blood

born to steal;___ Two com-mon thieves must pay___ for their mis-takes now our time has run out all tha'
that He shed;___ Gave Him-self as a sac-ri-fice___ now He stands___ in the gap be-tween Hell

left to do is hate.___ And the Man___ In The Mid-dle just keeps___ on giv-ing His love___ a-way;
and Par-a-dise.___

And a-bove___ the groans___ of the dy-ing He's cry-ing, "Come live with me___ to-day!"___

Still no-one sees___ that He's who He claims to be;___ And the Man___ In The Mid-dle keeps

(D.C.)

giv-ing His love___ a-way!___

MIGHTY FORTRESS

Words by JOHN CHISUM & BILL GEORG
Music by BILL GEORG

With energy

Je-sus is___ the Cap-tain of sal-va-tion

MANSION BUILDER

By ANNE HERR

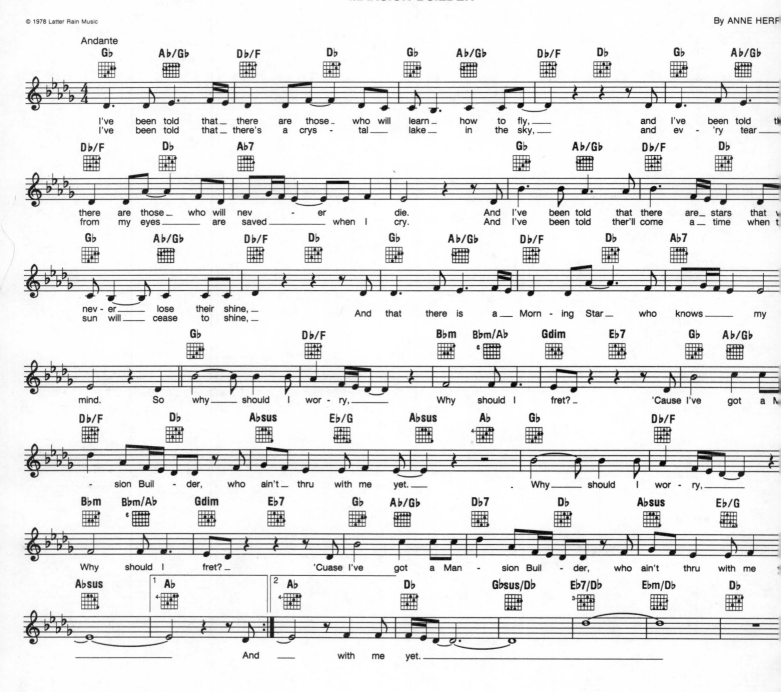

I've been told that there are those who will learn how to fly, and I've been told th
I've been told that there's a crys - tal lake in the sky, and ev - 'ry tear

there are those who will nev - er die. And I've been told that there are stars that w
from my eyes are saved when I die cry. And I've been told ther'll come a time when t

nev - er lose their shine, And that there is a Morn - ing Star who knows my
sun will cease to shine,

mind. So why should I wor - ry, Why should I fret? 'Cause I've got a M

- sion Buil - der, who ain't thru with me yet. Why should I wor - ry,

Why should I fret? 'Cuase I've got a Man - sion Buil - der, who ain't thru with me

And with me yet.

MESSIAH

By MIKE DEASY & PHIL DRISC

With a lively beat

Mes - si - ah, Prince of Peace,

Lord of Lords, Might - y God, King of Kings, Mes - si

- ah, let's go!

MELTDOWN
(At Madame Tussaud's)

By STEVE TAY[LOR]

MIRROR OF YOUR HEART

By DAVID C. MARTIN
& CHRIS CHRISTIAN

MIGHTY LORD

By PHIL MAD

MOUNTAIN TOP

ght © 1977 Bug and Bear Music
ively administered by LCS Music Group, Inc., P. O. Box 202406, Dallas TX 75220
y Permission

By BROWN BANNISTER

MIZPAH

Words and Music
BYRON WA...

I can't be-lieve that once a-gain it's time for us to go. ___ It seems like no time at all since we first said hel-lo.

Thank you all for com-ing, all my old friends and my new. Hap-pi-ness for me is when I sing my songs for you.

hope next time we have more time to spend. ___ So let me say in part-ing un-til we meet a-gain; May yo...

love flow like a foun-tain, ___ may your days be free of doubt. May your life be-come as ef-fort-less ___ as breath-ing in an...

out, May you al-ways com-plete what you be-gin. May you nev-er have so much that you're a slave to what you own, ___ May y...

al-ways have the wis-dom to leave well e-nough a-lone. When dark clouds close a-round you may you feel God's light...

round you when you pray. ___ When you need some-one to guide you may you know God walks be-side you all the way.

May you al-ways wake up cheer-ful ___ and give thanks for ev-'ry day, Know the love that you re-ceive comes from t...

love you give a-way. May your faith be a cush-ion when you fall. May you know you al-ways man-i-fest wh...

ev-er's in your mind. If good is what you're look-ing for ___ then good is what you find. When dark clouds close

round you may you feel God's light sur-round you when you pray. ___ When you need some-one

guide you may you know God walks be-side you all the way. Oh _____ When _____ you need some-one to

guide you may you know God walks be-side you all the way, _____ All the way. _____

THE MORE I KNOW OF YOU

By MARK BALDWIN, DICK TUNNEY
& PAUL SMITH

With a gentle beat

VERSE

1. Liv-ing ____ my days in ____ Your pres - ence, _____ each day ____ un -
2.(See additional lyrics)

like the one ___ be - fore. _____ Ev - ery page ___ I turn, all the

les-sons that ___ I learn _____ make me want ___ to know You e - ven more.

CHORUS

And The More I Know Of You, _____ the more I want ___ to be _____ a mir - ror of ___ Your heart

shin-ing end - less-ly. _____ Like a sun that nev - er dies, _____ they'll

see You in ___ my eyes. _____ Oh, Lord, The More I Know ___ Of You.

Additional Lyrics

2. Learning to walk in Your Spirit,
trust that every step I take
will drawe me nearer to You.
In all I say and do,
make me more like You, Lord I pray.
(Chorus)

MORE POWER TO YA

Words and Mu
BOB HART

MY FINEST HOUR
(You Have Been)

By GEORGE GAGLIARDI

MIRACLE MAN

Words and Music by DAVID R. LEH...
& CHARLES AARON WILB...

With a driving beat

Heal-ing lep-ers that cried, "Have pit-y on us." Giv-ing sight to Bar-ti-mae-us there in the dust, A wo-m...
heart-ache and pain are all a-round you. Troub-led wa-ters of life, al-most drown you,

came to the well with a buck-et you know but she left with a ri-ver in her soul.)
Just reach up to the reach-ing down hand. Yes, Je-sus is the Mir-a-cle Man. }

CHORUS

He'll give you a mir-a-cle He'll give you a mir-a-cle He'll give you

mir-a-cle Je-sus is the Mir-a-cle Man. When Giv-ing

sight to the blind and turn-in' wa-ter to wine it's all at His com-mand. Giv-in

life to a ru-ler's daught-er, calm-ing storms, walk-in' on wat-er, Yes, Je-sus is the Mir-a-cle Man. And

Fine

D.S. al

MY SOUL DESIRE

By MARK BALDWIN & NILES BO...

Reverently
VERSE

1. Lord, when You placed Your hands up-on me, I knew that I could
2. (See additional lyrics)

er be the same. For in that mo-ment I be-came Your ser-vant,

CHORUS

and still to-day I on-ly have one aim. My Sole De-sire

is to be used,— an emp-ty ves-sel long-ing to be filled by You. My Sole De-sire— is to serve You,— Lord, to do Your per-fect will. To work each day— and build— Your king-dom— Is— My Sole De-sire.

Additional Lyrics

2. Lord, I do not seek to claim the glory.
My wish is to be under Your control.
For I know that only You are worthy.
And it's You who placed this longing in my soul.

(CHORUS)

NOT OF THIS WORLD

Words and Music by
BOB HARTMAN

Gently, in two

We are pil - grims In a strange — land We are so — far from our
en - voys We must tar - ry With this mes - sage We must

home - land With each pass - ing day — it seems — so clear This world will nev - er want
car - ry There's so much to do — be - fore we leave With so man - y more who may
Je - sus told — us men would hate — us But we must be of —

— us here — We're not wel - come in — this world of wrong — We are for - eign - ers — who don't be -
— be - lieve Our mis - sion here can nev - er fail And the gates of hell will not pre -
— good cheer — he has o - ver - come this world of dark - ness And soon we will de - part from

long. ———
vail. ———
here. ———

We are strang - ers We are a - li - ens We are

Not Of This World, We are We are strang - ers We are

a - li - ens We are Not Of This World. ———

World. ———

To Coda

D.S. al Coda

CODA

NEW DAY

Words and Mus
TERRY TO

1. This new day's a-noth-er chance to be all that I can be A chance to pu
2. (See additional lyrics)

sue the dream that some-how e-lu-ded me This new day's a gift from God

who brought the Son my way He swept the night a-way

and blessed me with this New Day. There's some-thing a-bout a morn-ing

that's won-der-ful and new The sun gent-ly ris-ing burn-ing of th

dew While na-ture sings a pre-lude the sun ush-ers the night

to a room of wait-ing re-plac-ing it with light He swept th

night a-way and blessed me with this New Day.

Additional lyrics

VERSE 2: The night made empty promises
That it could never keep
And it leaves me longing for the dawn
For something I could see

Through the pain of night I knew
The sun was on his way
To bring me hope for life again
And bring me this new day.

MORE THAN WONDERFUL

By LANNY WO

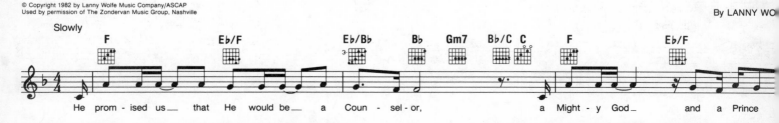

He prom-ised us that He would be a Coun-sel-or, a Might-y God and a Prince

A New Heart

By MICHAEL W. SMITH & MIKE HUD...

A NEW SONG

By NANCY, CINDY & BECKY CR...

Moderately

He made the birds to sing and bells to ring when I gave Him my heart He turned
hope back to me and set my soul free when I gave Him my heart He gave

gray skies to blue made the sun come shin-in' thru when I gave Him my heart So I'll sing from
words to a song to sing all day long when I gave Him my heart

CHORUS

NOT TO US, O LORD

By MICHAEL W. SMITH
& PAUL SMITH

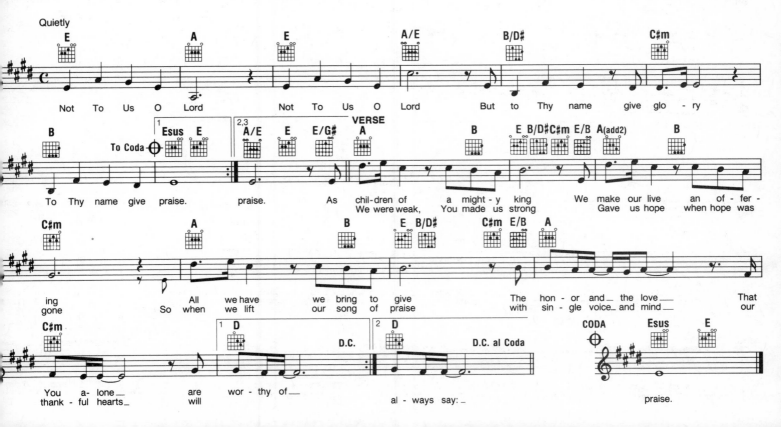

NO MORE NIGHT

By WALT HAR

NOT BY MIGHT, NOT BY POWER

By CHRIS CHRISTIAN
WILLIAM J. GAITHER & GLORIA GAITHER

NO OTHER NAME BUT JESUS

By CHRIS CHRIST
GARY McSPADDEN & BILLY SMI

NO SHORTAGE

By GARY S. PAXTON

all gon - na die, __ But I know a great thing that there's no short-age of, __ There's no short-age on _ God's mer-cy; There's no
air in the sky. __

short - age on __ God's love. God is love and mer - cy un - end - ing, __ His pre - cious love will leave you no doubt; __

__ When from sa - tan you need de - fend - ing, __ God has sup - plies __ that will nev - er run out. __

There's a short - age on friend - ship, there's a short - age on smiles, __ There's a short - age on neigh - bors, though there's

mil - lions for miles; __ Thank Hea - ven for one __ thing that there's no short - age of, __ There's no

short - age of __ God's mer - cy, there's no short - age of God's love, There's no short - age!

OH LORD YOU'RE BEAUTIFUL

By KEITH GREEN

Slowly

Oh, Lord, You're Beau - ti - ful. __ Your face is all I see. __ For when Your eyes are on this child, _ Your grace a - bounds to

me. Oh Lord, please light the fire __ that once burned bright and clear. __ Re - place the lamp of my first love that

burns with Ho - ly fear. __ I wan - na take Your Word and shine it all a - round. __ First help me just to live it,

Lord! __ And when I'm do - ing well, help me to nev - er seek a crown. __ For my re - ward is giv - ing glo - ry to You. Oh,

D.S. al Fine

The Now And The Not Yet

By PAM MARK HA...

O MAGNIFY THE LORD

By DICK TUNNEY
& MELODIE TUNNEY

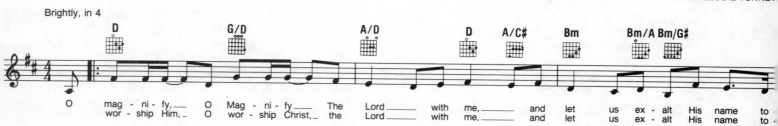

Now Or Never

By SI SIMONSON & TIM HOSM

OH BUDDHA

By MARK FARROW

NOTHING BUT THE BLOOD*—WASHED IN THE BLOOD**

*Words and Music by ROBERT LOW
**Words and Music by ELISHA A. HOFFM
Arrangement by STAN ENDICOTT & KELLY WILLA

Arrangement (as performed by Kelly Willard) © 1984 Willing Heart Music

Moderately with a beat

gar - ments_ spot - less, are they white as snow,_ are you washed_ in the blood_ of _ the lamb?_ Oh

oh,_ pre - cious is the flow _ that _ makes me white as _ snow, _

_ no _ oth - er _ fount I know, _ noth - ing but the blood of _

Je - sus._ Ah _

Are you washed _ in the_ blood?_ Oh _ Are you washed _

OVER THE MOUNTAIN

Words and Music by
CHARLENE CARTER

Moderately, with rhythm

1,4. Son's com - in' up_____ O - ver The Moun - tain. Son's com - in' up o - ver that moun - tain some - day.
2. Bird fly - in' high _ O - ver The Moun - tain. Bird fly - in' high, sing - in' a brand new song.
3. all _ rise _ in - to the Son's love. We all shall _ rise sing - in' a song_ of praise. But

Com - ing on a cloud_ in_ great glo - ry. Souls com - in' up o - ver that moun - tain some - day.
Sing - in' a song _ of praise and glo - ry. We all shall _ fly o - ver that moun - tain some - day.
'til that time we,ve got to climb, know - ing we'll all be o - ver that moun - tain some - day. Do you be -

lieve you will rise? Do you be - lieve you will fly? _ We _

CODA

day. Son's com - in' up_____ O - ver The Moun - tain. Son's com - in' up o - ver that moun - tain some - day.

O COME ALL YE FAITHFUL

By RICHARD MULLI

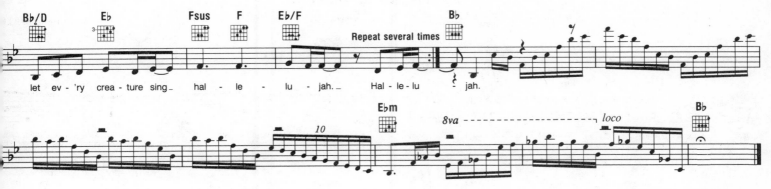

let ev-'ry creature sing_ hal-le-lu-jah._ Hal-le-lu jah.

ONE THING LEADS TO ANOTHER

By LEON PATILLO

Steadily

One Thing Leads To An-oth-er, be it bad_ or be it_ good._ One Thing Leads To An-

-oth-er, it's a life-long road a-head._

Some-times it just seems im-pos-si-ble._
So you want to play hide and seek,_
So you feel you've been blessed in life,_

to say a sim-ple thing_ like_ "no."
good by day bad by night.
won-der-ing_ how to re-pay.

To stand up for your prin-ci-ples_
What you do in the se-cret place_
Stick your light way up on the hill._

hap-pens to ev-ery-one I know.
shall come out in the light.
so oth-ers might_ find the way.

To Coda ⊕

One Thing Leads To An-oth-er, be it bad_ or

be it_ good._ You won't be hap-py_ there_ that's no-where for you._

Life has so much in_ store_ so much_ more_ for you.

D.S. al Coda

CODA

One Thing Leads To An-oth-er, be it bad_ or be it_ good._ One Thing Leads To An-

Repeat ad lib. | Ending

-oth-er it's a life-long road a-head._ road a-head._

O HOLY ONE

By MARTY GO
(Based on Psalm

pon a cross is the heal-ing of our lives. _____ O Ho-ly One, I de-

light to do your will. Our shame Je-sus took, now we're near not far a-part. And lo I

come, know-ing no peace un-til my name's in your book, and your law's in my heart.

And lo I come, hold-ing fast and hold-ing still, my

name in your book, and your love in my heart. _____

ON MY WAY

By PHILLIP SANDIFER

On My Way Your love will guide__ me On My Way I'll seek Your light__ On My Way I'll al-ways call up-on__ Your__

name. And if ev-er I am blind-ed__ I'll de-pend up-on__ Your sight On My Way Your love will guide__ me__ On My

Way. { Well I set my eyes up-on__ You__ And I walk with-in__ Your grace
(See additional lyrics)

want-ing to be with you Lord__ ev-en long-ing for the day And as I stand with-in Your door-way now__ I can

feel You draw-ing near But You've told me there's a rea-son for me__ here And On My fall. And On My

(Repeat Chorus)
D.S. al Fine

Additional Lyrics

2. Well the battle, it lies before us
   But the victor goes ahead
   Singing unto the nations
   To accept the Word we spread
   And the Holy name of Jesus

Will echo as our call
And will cause the feeble
Gates of hell to fall...

(CHORUS 2 times)

OH, HOW HE LOVES YOU AND ME

By KURT KAIS

ON THE WATER

By MARTY McCA
& VICKIE McCA

Additional Lyrics

2. He speaks my name in the moonlight
I reach out to take His hand
Then I hear His mighty voice
Calling me to stand.

(CHORUS)

ON AND ON
(Love Song)

By AMY GRANT
& BROWN BANNISTER

OLD MAN'S RUBBLE

Copyright © 1977 Bug and Bear Music
Exclusively administered by LCS Music Group, Inc., P. O. Box 202406, Dallas TX 75220
Used by Permission

By BROWN BANNIS

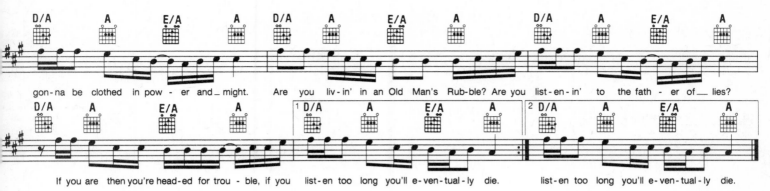

gon-na be clothed in pow-er and_might. Are you liv-in' in an Old Man's Rub-ble? Are you list-en-in' to the fath-er of lies?

If you are then you're head-ed for trou-ble, if you list-en too long you'll e-ven-tual-ly die.   list-en too long you'll e-ven-tual-ly die.

OPEN ARMS

By AMY GRANT, GARY CHAPMAN,
& BRUCE HIBBARD

Relaxed, with a beat

I guess I got a lot of learn-ing to do__ A-bout the way that you love__
On-ly yes-ter-day the thought came to me Is your love as deep as they say

If it had been left up to me I gave my love__ a long time a-go__ But
Won-der where those ques-tions come from__ Soon as I learn___ I'll chase them a-way__ 'Cause

you got a way of woo-ing me__ Ten-der and true___ And though I don't de-serve__ it__ I'm
I've had a taste of ten-der-ness__ Sim-ple and true____ It drives a-way the doubt-ing__ And

fall-ing in-to___ your } O-pen__ Arms__ Your love has tak-en__ hold and I can't fight it I'm
draws me in-to___ your {

giv-ing__ in-to your O-pen__ Arms__ They pull me to you They wrap your love a-round_me I'll

rest in your O-pen Arms _____   rest in your O-pen Arms__

O-pen Arms __ your love__ has tak-en hold and I can't fight it I'm giv-ing in-to your

Repeat and Fade

O-pen Arms __ they pull me to you They wrap your love a-round me I'll rest in your o-pen___

On One Condition

By NAN GUR
& MELODIE TUN

Additional Lyrics

2. Dear Heavenly Father
Aren't You happy to have
A dedicated Christian like me
Someone who's willing to serve
Holding nothing back
One who lives unselfishly
'Cause when it comes to giving
Everything to You
There ain't no competition
I'll always keep You first
In everything I do
But only On One Condition

Chorus

PEOPLE IN A BOX

By ED DeGARMO, DANA KEY & BOB FARRELL

Moderately with a Funky Beat

ONE LAST GOODBYE

By LARRY BRYANT, LESA BRY.
DEBBIE FRANCO & KEITH THO

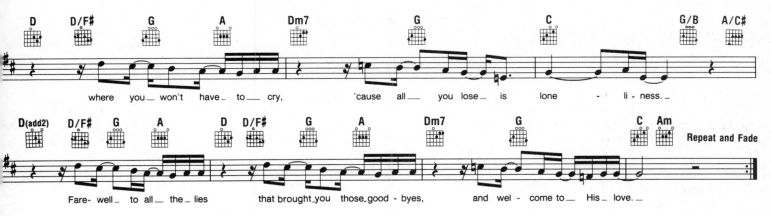

where you_ won't have to_ cry, 'cause all_ you lose is lone - li - ness._

Fare- well_ to all_ the_ lies that brought_you those_good - byes, and wel - come to_ His_ love._

Repeat and Fade

ORDINARY PEOPLE

'7 Danniebelle Music/Birdwing Music/Cherry Lane Music Publishing Co., Inc.

By DANNIEBELLE HALL

Just Or-di-nar-y Peo-ple, God us-es Or-di-nar-y Peo-ple He choos-es peo-ple just like me and you_ who are

will-ing to do as He____ com-mands. God us-es peo-ple_ that will give Him all, ___ no mat-ter

how small your all___ may seem to you; ___ be-cause lit-tle_ be-comes much as you place it in the Mas-ter's

hand. Just Or-di-nar-y Oh, just like that lit-tle lad who gave_ Je-sus all he had; how the

mul-ti-tude was fed with a fish and loaves of bread! What you have may not seem much, but when you

yield it to the touch___ of the Mas-ter's lov-ing hand then you will un-der-stand how your

life could nev-er be the same. Just Or-di-nar-y place it in the Mas-ter's hand._ Yeah._

D.S. al Coda

CODA

Oh, your lit-tle be-comes much as you place it in the Mas-ter's hand. ___

ONE MORE SONG FOR YOU

By MICHAEL & STORMIE OMAR

ONLY CHILD

Words and Musi
VIC CLAY & TERRY TO

PRAISE THE LORD, HE NEVER CHANGES

right 1974, © Copyright 1975 by Word Music (A Div. of WORD, INC.)
by Permission

By STORMIE OMARTIAN
& RON HARRIS

PASSIN' THE FAITH ALONG

By JON M

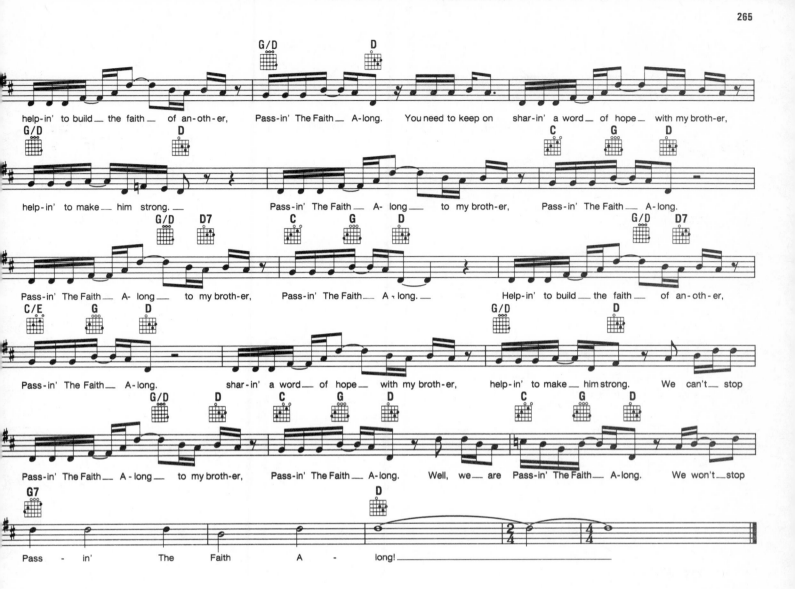

POUR ON THE POWER

By DWIGHT LILES,
MARK GERSMEHL & NILES BOROP

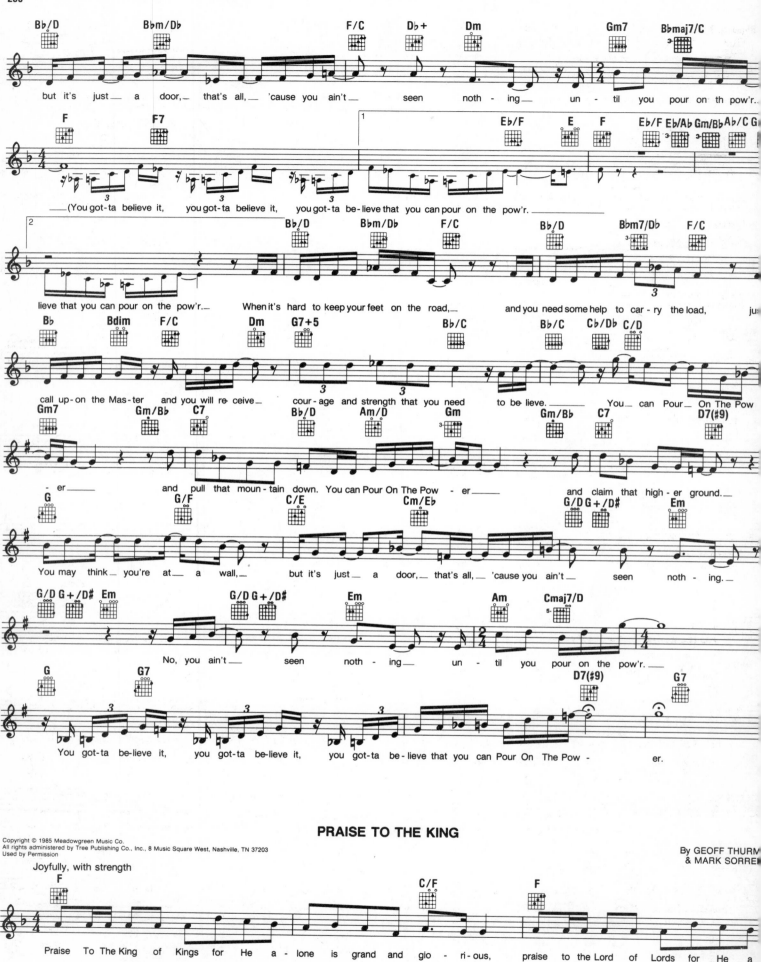

PRAISE TO THE KING

By GEOFF THURM
& MARK SORREI

Joyfully, with strength

Praise To The King of Kings for He a - lone is grand and glo - ri - ous, praise to the Lord of Lords for He a

lone will reign vic - to - ri - ous. Praise To The King of our sal - va - tion, praise to the Lord of right - eous - ness, praise to the God of new cre - a - tion

PEOPLE NEED THE LORD

Words and Music by
PHILL McHUGH & GREG NELSON

PROMISES

Words and Music by
TANYA GOODMAN & MICHAEL SYKES

PRAY FOR ME

Words and Mus
CHARLES AARON WILB
B.J. THOMAS & GLORIA THO

PROCLAIM THE GLORY OF THE LORD

By DWIGHT LILES & NILES BO

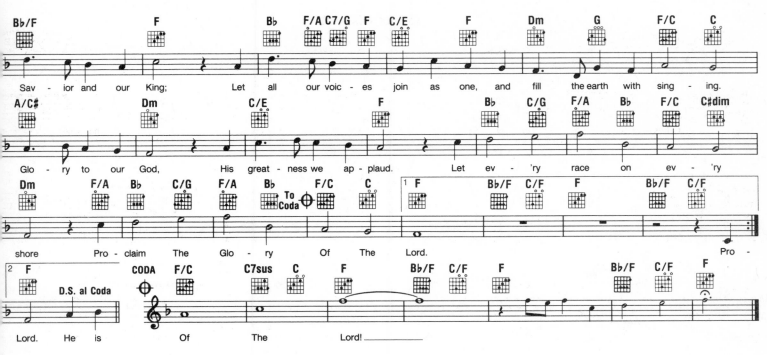

Savior and our King; Let all our voic-es join as one, and fill the earth with sing-ing.

Glo-ry to our God, His great-ness we ap-plaud. Let ev-'ry race on ev-'ry

shore Pro-claim The Glo-ry Of The Lord. Pro-

Lord. He is Of The Lord!

REJOICE

73 Sandtree Music/Birdwing Music/Cherry Lane Music Publishing Co., Inc.

By PHIL KEAGGY

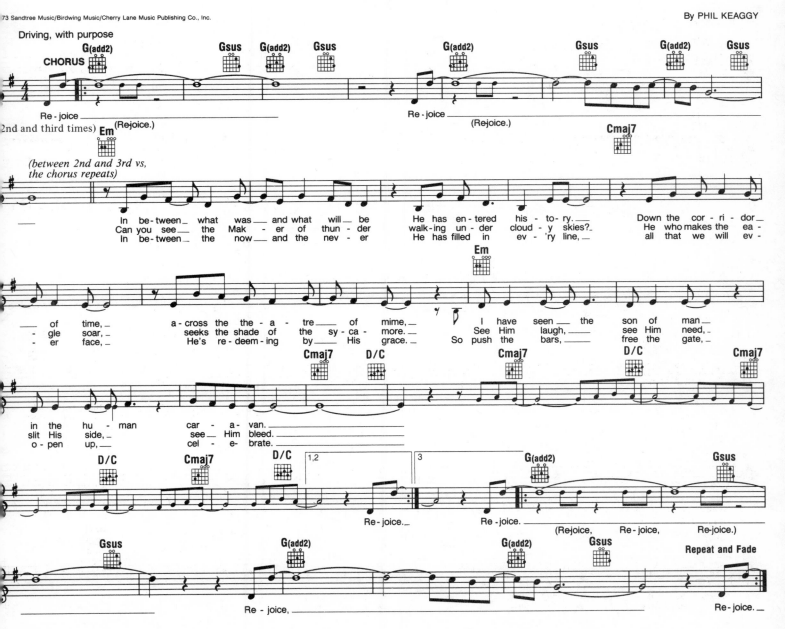

Driving, with purpose

CHORUS

Re-joice _____ Re-joice _____
(Rejoice.) (Rejoice.)

(2nd and third times)

(between 2nd and 3rd vs, the chorus repeats)

In be-tween_ what was_ and what will be He has en-tered his-to-ry.___ Down the cor-ri-dor_
Can you see_ the Mak-er of thun-der walk-ing un-der cloud-y skies?_ He who makes the ea-
In be-tween_ the now_ and the nev-er He has filled in ev-'ry line, _ all that we will ev-

of time, _ a-cross the the-a-tre_ of mime, _ I have seen_ the son of man
-gle soar, _ seeks the shade of the sy-ca-more._ See Him laugh, _ see Him need,
-er face, _ He's re-deem-ing by His grace. So push the bars, _ free the gate,

in the hu-man car-a-van._____ I
slit His side, _ see Him bleed._____ o-pen up, _ cel-e-brate. _____

Re-joice._ Re-joice. (Rejoice, Re-joice, Re-joice.)

Repeat and Fade

Re-joice, _____ Re-joice. ___

THE PRODIGAL
(I'll Be Waiting)

By GARY CHAPMAN, AMY GRANT
& ROBBIE BUCHANAN

REVIVE US, OH LORD

Birdwing Music/Some-O-Dat Music [Administered by Dayspring Music (a div. of Word, Inc.)]

By STEVE CAMP & CARMAN LICCIARDELLO

QUIET LOVE

By BILLY SMILEY & MARK GERSM

Gently

Soft as a whis - per of ____ a morn - ing breeze ____ And warm like the s
Sweet as the song ____ a moth - er sings to her child, And fresh like the mo

- light shin - ing through ____ sum - mer trees. ____ Oh ____ Lord ____ flow thro
- tain flow - ers grow - in' wild. ____

me. Come plant your ____ seed, ____ Spir - it move ____ with - in ____ me

Give me what I need, ____ Qui - et Love, Qui - et Love. ____

kind of love ____ that needs no words ____ to show that it is there. Qui - et Love,
kind of love ____ that reach - es out ____ when no one else is there,

Qui - et Love. ____ A love ____ that needs no rea - son to
A love ____ that lis - tens to the cries tha

show it cares, Qui - et Love.
no one hears,

QUIET PLACE

Words and Music
DON JAR\

Slowly

1,3. Sun is set, the day is done. The bat - tle's been fought and the vic - to - ry won.
2. How I long to meet You here, lay at ____ your feet all my fears.

To Coda

And now ____ it's time to slow the pace, re - new my strength in this Qui - et Place.
You ____ were there as I ran the race. You brought me back to this Qui - et Place.

RIGHT WHERE YOU ARE

By PAUL SMITH
& KEITH THOMAS

THE RACE IS ON

By MICHAEL W. SM
& DEBORAH D. SM

RESIDENT POWER

Words and Music
CHARLES AARON WILBU

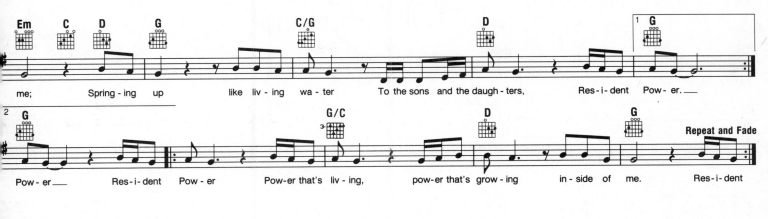

me;   Spring-ing up   like liv-ing wa-ter To the sons and the daugh-ters, Res-i-dent Pow-er.___

Pow-er___   Res-i-dent Pow-er   Pow-er that's liv-ing,   pow-er that's grow-ing in-side of me.   Res-i-dent

Repeat and Fade

THE ROAD TO ZION

By MICHAEL HUDSON

Slowly, with much meaning

There is a way that leads to life, the few that find it nev-er die, past moun-tain peaks graced white with
runs be-side the road, its wa-ters liv-ing as they flow, in li-quid voice the wa-ter

snow the way goes bright-er as it goes. There is a road in-side of you, in-side of me there is one
calls on thirst-y knees the Pil-grim falls.

too, no stum-bling Pil-grim in the dark, the Road To Zi-on's in your heart. The Road To Zi-on's in your

heart. The riv-er Some-times it's good, to look back down,

we've gained such ground. Joy is not in where we've been, He's wait-ing at the end. There is a

road in-side of you, in-side of me there is one too, no stum-bling Pil-grim in the dark, the Road To

Zi-on's in your heart. There is a Zi-on's in your heart. The Road To Zi-on's in your heart, the Road To

Zi-on's in your heart.

Raining On The Inside

By AMY GRANT & KATHY TROCC

Gently

When all good-byes__ are said and done__ and night-time finds__ you home__ Are you all right__

spend a night__ of be-ing all__ a-lone Or do you hide__ be-tween the lines__

con-ver-sa-tions past__ A wall of words__ a heart un-heard__ that hides be-hind_____

mask I'm___ Rain-ing__ On The In-side My heart wells up with tears__ that start to pour_____ But when I

___ Rain-ing__ On The In-side Then your cries of love break thru and I fall in love with you once____ more__

When friends who care__ can't be there__ to ease a-way my pain__

peace of mind__ is hard to find__ like sun-light in__ the rain God sees my heart__ the deep-est part__

side this lone-ly me__ And reach-in' in__ His love be-gins__ to heal the heart__

me I'm__ Rain-ing__ On The In-side My heart wells up with tears__ that start to pour_____ But when I'

___ Rain-ing__ On The In-side Then your cries of love break thru and I fall in love with you once____ more__

ROCK SOLID

By RAYMOND BROWN

Right Direction

Words and Music
JOE HUFFMAN & DAVID R. LEHM

ques - tion in____ my mind.____ Je - sus walks be - fore____ me, and I'm go - in' to the oth - er side.____

D.S. al Coda   **CODA**

_____ Cause' I'm Head - ed in the Right Di - rec - tion.____   **Repeat and Fade**

RUNNER

Words by TWILA & STARLA PARIS
Music by TWILA PARIS

Cou - ri - er val - iant bear - ing the flame____ Mes - sen - ger no - ble sent in his name____
Ob - sta - cle an - cient chill - ing the way____ En - e - my wak - ened stok - ing the fray____

Fast - er and hard - er run through the night____ Des - per - ate re - lay car - ry the light, ____ car - ry the light. ____
Still be de - ter - mined fear - less and true____ Lift high the stand - ard car - ry it through, ____ car - ry it through. ____

Run - ner,____ when the road is long____ feel like giv - ing in, ____ But you're hang - in' on____ Oh, Run - ner,____ when the

race is won____ you will run in - to____ His arms. ____   **To Coda**

CODA

Mind - ful of man - y wait - ing to run

____ des - tined to fin - ish what you've be - gun, ____ Mil - lions be - fore____ you cheer - ing you on____ God - speed, dear Run -

- ner, car - ry it home, _____ car - ry it home. ____   Run - ner,____ when the

road is long____ feel like giv - ing in, ____ But you're hang - in' on, ____ Oh, Run - ner,____ when the race is won____ you will

run in - to____ His arms. ____

RISE AGAIN

By DALLAS H

RUN WITH THE POWER

Words and Musi
CHARLES AARON WILB

SAILING ON THE SEA OF YOUR LOVE

THE RED SEA PARTED

By PHILL McHUGH & GREG NEL

Moderately

Dark wa-ters lay be-fore them, dark forc-es came be-hind, to their left and right the de-sert brought pan-ic to their minds.

e-vil of that hour ___ was strong-er than the sun that beat on them with no-where left to run.

char-i-ots of E-gypt drew near-er as they cried, yet Mos-es stood there calm-ly with a fear-less faith in-side.

said there is a pow-er far great-er than ___ the sword, stand still and you will wit-ness a might-y sal-va-tion from

Lord. And then The Red Sea Part-ed for now there was a way to en-ter in

joic-ing to vic-to-ry that day. Yes, then The Red Sea Part-ed, at last they could

free with Pha-raoh's ar-my bur-ied in the sea.

ta-tion came be-side me and it told its fin-est lies, mak-ing all the dark-er pleas-ures so ___ pleas-ant to my eyes.

knew a lack of pray-ing had led me to that hour stand-ing there sur-round-ed by sin's pow'r.

ter-ror of those mo-ments be-gan to fade a-way, as my heart re-called God's mer-cies are ___ all new ev-'ry day. And

spir-it took its ar-mor as my lips took up ___ the sword. Light broke through the dark-ness, a might-y sal-va-tion from

SOMEBODY'S BROTHER

By GREG NELSON
& SCOTT WESLEY BROWN

SAFE

By JEREMY DAL

SHEPHERD OF MY HEART

By MARK BALDWIN & DICK TUNNEY

Additional Lyrics

2. Keeper of this heart of mine your patience has no end
You've loved me back into your arms time and time again
So if I start to wander like a lamb that's gone astray
I'll trust in you. Shepherd of my heart

3. Giver of this live in me, You're what I'm living for
For all my deepest gratitude you love me even more
So as I walk through valley's listening for the Master's call
I'll trust in you. Shepherd of my heart

SAIL ON

By CHRIS CHR...

Calypso

Sail On___ when the wa - ter gets high___ Sail On___ when the wind___ starts to die___ Sail

___ It's just a mat - ter of min - utes till His ship comes to get___ us and we'll all get in___ it

{ When we're all born___ We set set out to sea___ Look - ing for an - swers con - tin - u - ous-ly___
Cast up your sails___ And let the wind blow___ Je - sus will never let your ship lose con - trol___

Then when we find out to Him we be - long___ We watch for the signs and keep sail - in' on___ Sa
Just keep your com - pass set on the sun.___ He'll guide you safe - ly to his

beau - ti - ful home. We can't af - ford___ to throw our lives___ to the wind___ We got the Lord___ in

trol of our ship.___ And He'll guide us safe - ly in___ He'll get us in_____ Sail

On___ when the wa - ter gets high___ Sail On___ When the wind starts to die___ Sail

___ It's just a mat - ter of min - utes till His ship comes to get___ us and we'll all get in___ it. Sail

SCANDALON

By MICHAEL

Slowly

The se - ers and the proph - ets had___ fore - told___ it long a - go,___ that the long a - wait - ed One would make m
long the path of life___ there lies this stub - born scan - dal-on,___ and all who come___ this way___ must be

stum - ble;_____ but they were look - ing for a king to con - quer and___ to kill.___ Who'd
fend - ed.___ To some He is a bar - ri - er,___ to oth - ers He's the way;___

SHARAYAH

By AMY GRANT & CHRIS E

SHINE DOWN

By BILLY SMI
MARK GERSMEHL & BOB FARR

SO GLAD

By AMY GRANT, BROWN BANNISTER
& CHRIS CHRISTIAN

SHOPPING LIST

By LARRY BRYANT & LESA BRY...

With tongue in cheek

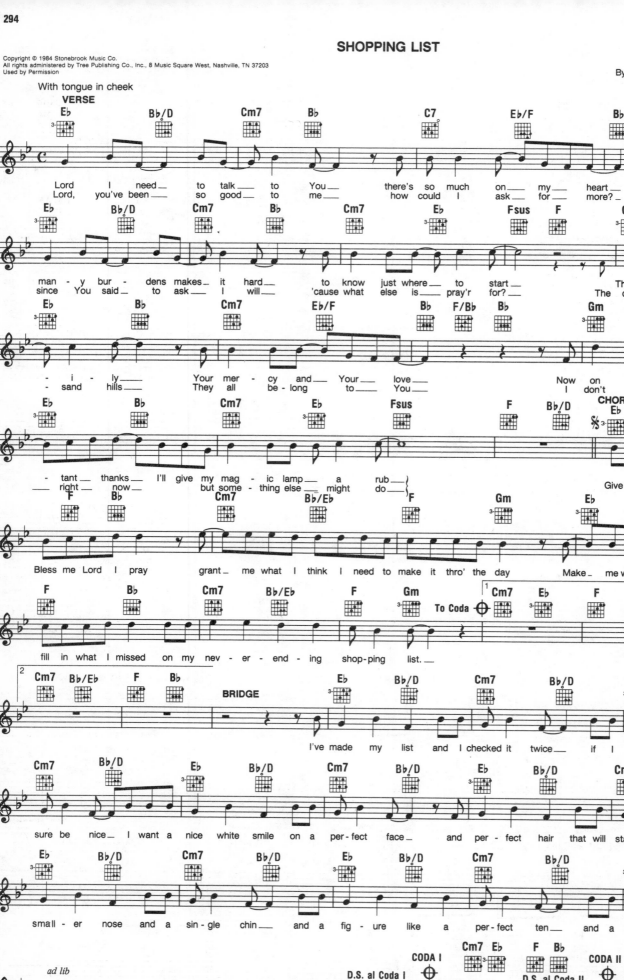

Lord I need to talk to You there's so much on my heart how could I ask for more?
Lord, you've been so good to me how could I ask for more?

man-y bur-dens makes it hard to know just where to start Thank You for Your fa...
since You said to ask I will 'cause what else is pray'r for? The cat-tle on the

-i-ly Your mer-cy and Your love Now on to more im-po...
-sand hills They all be-long to You I don't need an-y c...

-tant thanks I'll give my mag-ic lamp a rub
right now but some-thing else might do Give me this I want th...

Bless me Lord I pray grant me what I think I need to make it thro' the day Make me wealth-y keep me health-y

fill in what I missed on my nev-er-end-ing shop-ping list.

BRIDGE

I've made my list and I checked it twice if I got it all it wo...

sure be nice I want a nice white smile on a per-fect face and per-fect hair that will stay in place I want

small-er nose and a sin-gle chin and a fig-ure like a per-fect ten and a Mom that nev-er

ad lib

D.S. al Coda I

CODA I

CODA II

D.S. al Coda II

yells and screams, and hips that fit in designer jeans, and a tennis court
and a heated pool, I can use them Lord, as a witnessing tool -
And a color TV and a VCR, and Jesus plates on a brand new car!

SILENT LOVE

By ROBBIE BUCHANAN, PAUL & ELIZABETH JANZ,
RUSS & TORRI TAFF, CRISSIE GROSSMAN-PUIG

SILENT PARTNER

By ED DeGARMO, DANA
& JESSY DIX

SINCERELY YOURS

By GARY CHAPMAN

SILENT WEEPER

By GREG DAVIS & ANGIE LEWIS

1

2

Fm   G   Cm   Ab

dreams a - bout chang - ing the past, He knows that can't hap - pen. And the
won - ders if he is the on - ly Si - lent Weep - er.

Eb   Dsus   D/F#   Gm   Gm/F   Eb   Bb   Bb/D   Eb

Si - lent Weep - er don't give up on love. _____ There's no need to fear, _____ for the

Bb   F   Eb   Dsus   D   Gm   Gm/F   Eb

Lord is near. Si - lent Weep - er, Je - sus still loves you. _____ He can

Bb   Eb   Eb/G   Bb   Bb/D   Eb   Eb/G   Bb   Bb/D   Eb   Eb/G

heal your heart, for He, too, has scars, _____ and He knows how sor - row

Bb   Eb/Bb   Bb7   Gm   Ab   Bb

To Coda

feels. Day af - ter day _____ they take more of the blame as they bu - ry them - selves in the mem -

Eb   Ab   Bb   Cm   Bb   Ab   G7   Cm

- ories, And no - bod - y knows how far sor - row goes through the heart of the Si - lent Weep - er. _____

Cm   Ab   Cm   Ab   C(no3rd)

CODA

D.S. al Coda   *Play 8 times*

And the Si - lent Weep - er.

SWEET ADORATION

Copyright © 1980 Bug and Bear Music
Exclusively administered by LCS Music Group, Inc., P. O. Box 202406, Dallas TX 75220
Used by Permission

By BROWN BANNISTER,
LYNN SUTTER & DAWN RODGERS

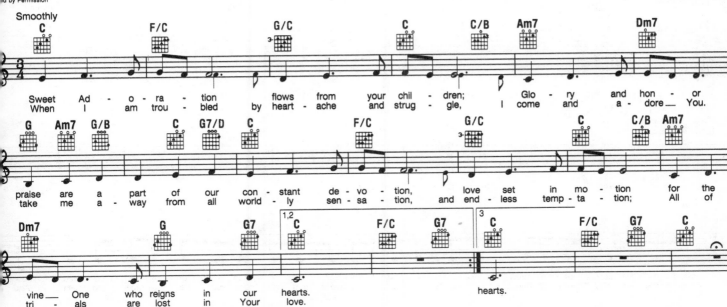

Smoothly

C   F/C   G/C   C   C/B   Am7   Dm7

Sweet Ad - o - ra - tion flows from your chil - dren; Glo - ry and hon - or and
When I am trou - bled by heart - ache and strug - gle, I come and a - dore _____ You. You

G   Am7   G/B   C   G7/D   C   F/C   G/C   C   C/B   Am7

praise are a - part of our con - stant de - vo - tion, love set in mo - tion for the Di -
take me a - way from all world - ly sen - sa - tion, and end - less temp - ta - tion; All of my

Dm7   G   G7   **1,2**   C   F/C   G7   **3**   C   F/C   G7   C

vine _____ One who reigns in our hearts.
tri - als are lost in Your love.   hearts.

SING THE GLORY OF HIS NAME

By TRICIA WA

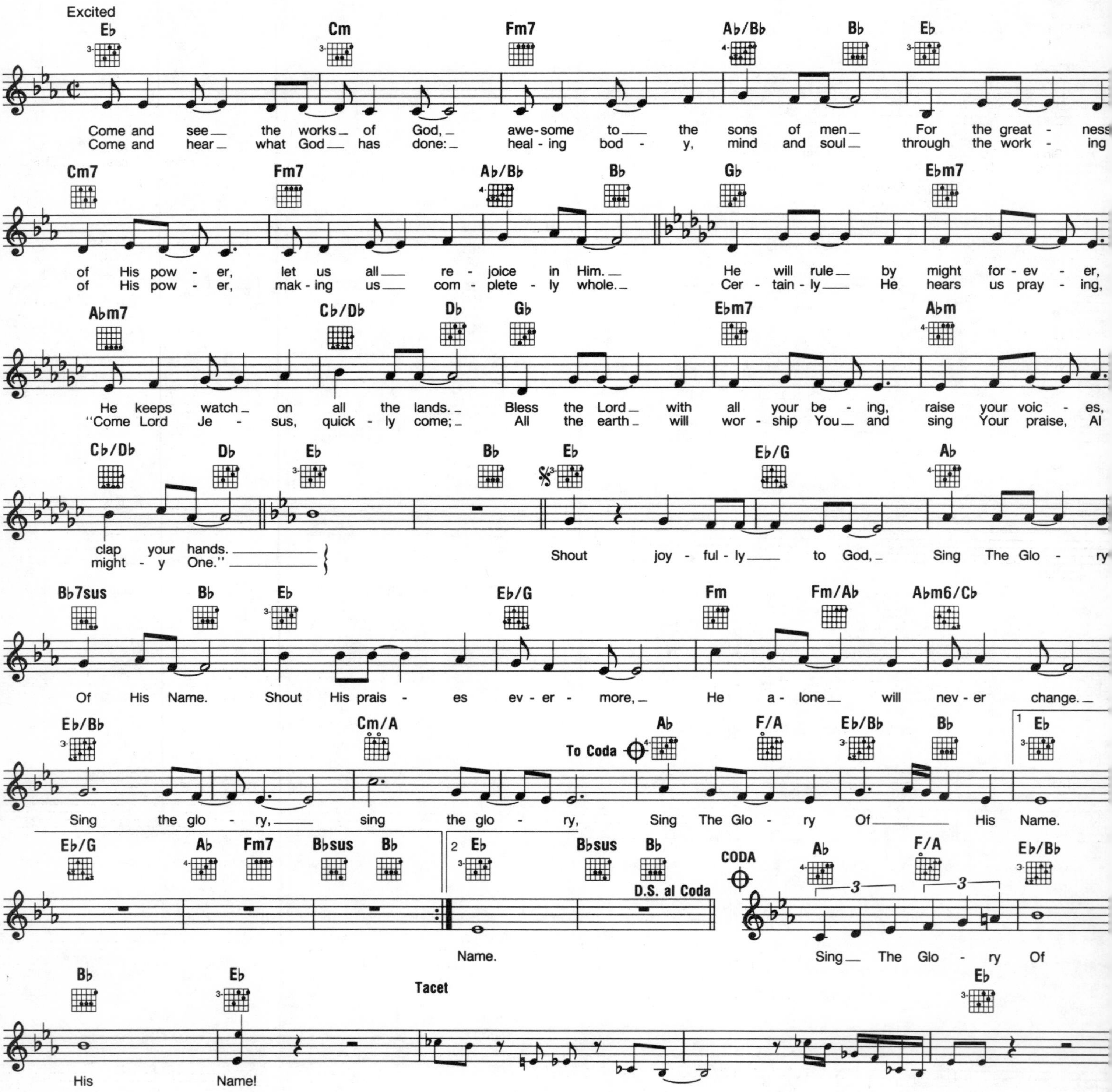

SING TO THE LORD

Words and Music by
ROBERT STERLING

With excitement and joy

SING UNTO HIM

By MICHAEL W. S

SING YOUR PRAISE TO THE LORD

By RICHARD MUL

SINGING A LOVE SONG

By JIM WEBER

SIX, SIX, SIX

By ED DeGARMO & DANA

Additional Lyrics

2. (Said that) things will be much better for tonight is new AG.
I can even change the weather and the things you won't believe.
I've got signs and wonders in my bag of tricks.
I demanded explanation, he just smiled and told me six, six, six.

3. When morning came I laughed at what I thought was just a dream.
Then I went to call my neighbor and just tell him all I'd seen.
When I reached for my address book I felt sick (so sick).
'Cause written 'cross the pages every number there was six, six, six.

A SONG FOR YOU

By CYNTHIA CLAWSON
& PATTY CLAWSON BERRY

THE SKY'S THE LIMIT

By LEON PA

SOMEBODY'S PRAYIN'

By JOHN ELLI

SOON AND VERY SOON

By ANDRAE CROUCH

3. No more dyin' there, we are goin' to see the King,
No more dyin' there, we are goin' to see the King,
No more dyin' there, we are goin' to see the King,
Hallelujah, we're goin' to see the King!
Hallelujah, etc. . . . .

THE SINGER

Words and Mu
LONNA M

Prayerfully

What d'-ya want to do to-night Lord What d'-ya got in mind for me We can work on a tune to-geth-er

sing a new har-mon-y You know You've giv-en all Your mus-ic to the child that won't re - fuse it I know

gave me all the songs I'd ev - er need Now I know there are a lot of sing-ers and
nev - er known a-no-ther po-et who's

lot of peo-ple writ-in' rhyme There's a lot of real good play-ers com-pos-ers keep-in' time And
au-thor and the min-strel too one who'll lay all the scores be-fore me with all the ly-rics cre-a-ted too As

just a-no-ther sing-er but Your mu-sic will al-ways ling-er ling-er with Your prais-es deep with-in my mind You're
duct-or You go be-fore us like the ver-ses be-fore a cho-rus You're the on-ly mu-sic mak-er in me

light You're the spot-light on the sing-er You're the light You're the glo-ry in this song So to-night

give back to You a sing-er for the light that has warmed me for so long Lord I'll

sing for You fea-tur-ing You just as long just as long as there's a song

Fine   D.S. al

I've

STILL ROLLS THE STONE

Words and Mus
BOB BENN

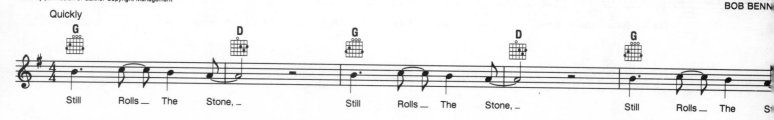

Quickly

Still Rolls The Stone, Still Rolls The Stone, Still Rolls The S

SO GLAD I KNOW

Words by DENIECE WII
Music by JAY GRUSKA & DENIECE WII

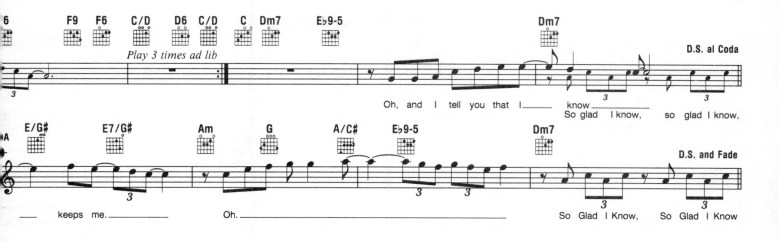

SOUND HIS PRAISE

By MELODIE TUNNEY

SOMEBODY BELIEVED

By GARY & ROSEMARY DU

Bb Cm7 Bb/D C#dim Cm Eb/F

Some-one dared to take the Good__ Lord at His word._____ Some - bo - dy Be-lieved.

Bb7 Eb7 Edim

Some - bo - dy Be - lieved.__ Some - bo - dy Be - lieved.__ Some - bo - dy Be - lieved._____ And God

Cm7 Dm7 Eb Eb/F Eb Bb Cm7 Dm7

moved His mighty - y hand__ when Some - bo - dy Be - lieved.__ Some - bo - dy Be - lieved.__ Yeah, God moved His might - y hand__

Eb Eb/F Bbm7/Eb Eb/F Bb B7 Bb7

_____ but Some - bo - dy Be - lieved,__ Some - bo - dy, Some - bo - dy Be - lieved._____

SPECIAL DELIVERY

By RON & CAROL HARRIS

Prayerfully

G Bm7 D C Am7 C Bm Am D C G Am7

RSE

3/4

Nev - er was an - y - one like Him, _____ nev - er will one be the same. _____
when I'm called; I will go glad - ly, _____ I will not grieve for the past,

G Bm7 D C Am7 C Bm Am C Bm Am C Bm C D7

CHORUS

Ti - ny babe, in - fant King, Sav - ior,_____ we wor - ship and hon - or the pow'r of His name. Oh, He came
for I know where I'll be go - ing._____ And I will be go - ing to see Him at last. I'm go - ing

G Bm G7 F G7 C Em Bm7 Am7 C Bm Am

spe - cial __ de - liv - er - y, __ wrapped up in love, bound by a prom - ise, sealed by a dove; __ and

G Bm G7 F G7 C Em Em7 A7sus A7 Am Bm D7 1.Am

To
Coda

filled with the Spir - it, car - ried by grace, {you knew where He was go - ing__ by the look on His face. __
{you'll know where I am go - ing__ by the look on my

G 2.G G CODA Am Bm D7 Am G

D.S. al Coda

And face. I'm go - ing look on my face._____ look on my face._____

SPARROW WATCHER

By PAM MARK
& RICHARD MU

Additional Lyrics

2. Jesus, our Brother
Dresser of the fields
Greeter of the morning
Who keeps the waters still

3. Judge between the nations
Turn our hearts from wrong
We join with all creation
And pray Thy kingdom come.

(CHORUS)

SPREADING ALL OVER THE WORLD

By WENDELL BU

STRENGTH OF MY LIFE

By LESLIE PHILLIPS

SPREADIN' LIKE WILDFIRE

Words and M
HAL NEWMAN & RACHEL NE

STAR OF THE MORNING

By LEON PA

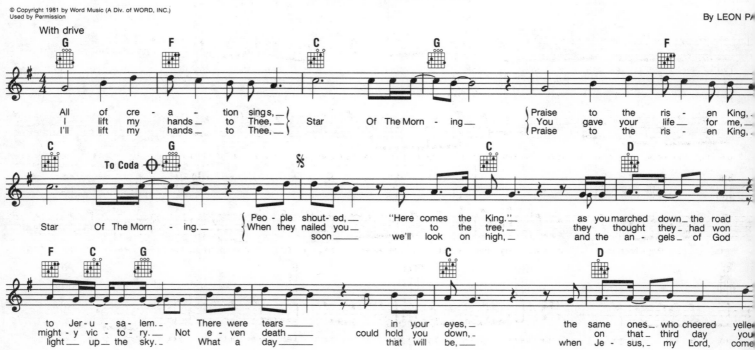

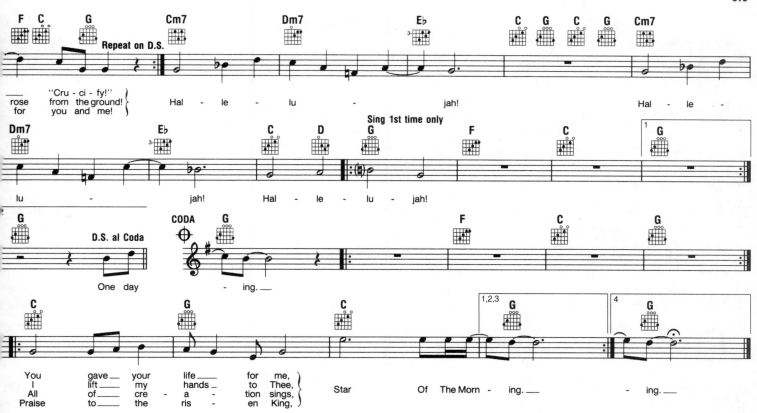

STUBBORN LOVE

By MICHAEL W. SMITH, GARY CHAPMAN,
SLOAN TOWNER, AMY GRANT & BROWN BANNISTER

STRAIGHT AHEAD

By MICHAEL W. S.
GARY CHAPMAN & AMY

STRANGER TO HOLINESS

By STEVE CAMP & ROB FR

STRONGER THAN THE WEIGHT

By DAVID C. M.
& DWIGHT

SURRENDER

By CLAIRE CLONINGER & BILL PURSE

Take Him To Heart

By DAVID C. M

TAKIN' THE EASY WAY

By ANNE HERRING

TAPESTRY

By TERI DeSARIO
& BILL

THY WORD

By MICHAEL W. SMITH & AMY GRANT

TEACH ME TO SEE

Words and Mus
CHARLES AARON WILBURN & GLORIA THO

THE TIME IS NOW

By MICHAEL OMARTIAN & STORMIE OMART

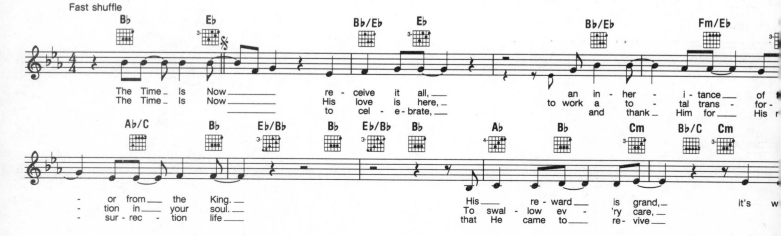

THAT'S WHEN THE ANGELS REJOICE

By LARRY BR

With a cut-time "feel"

At the com-ple-tion of the Gold-en Gate, no, the an-gels did not ce-le-brate, and when
light-bulb first lit up the town, no, the an-gles did not dance a-round, and when
Mod-el "T" first hit the street, it did-n't bring all heav-en to it's feet, and when

Wright boys flew their bird, no an-gel-ic shouts were heard.
man stepped on the Moon, they did-n't sing a vic-t'ry tune.
first com-put-er was born, they did-n't blow ol' Ga-briel's horn.

There's on-ly one thing that we're sure a-bout that can make those an-gels jump and shout, it's when a sin-ner makes the L

his choice, That's When The An-gels Re-joice. Now when the Now heav-en does-n't strike up the b

for an-y old oc-ca-sion at hand, it's got-ta be a spe-cial thing to

make those an-gels sing. Now when the Now when the Un-it-ed States be

came a na-tion, there was no an-gel-ic ce-le-bra-tion, when one lost sin-ner comes back home,

jump for joy a-round the throne. There's on-ly one thing that we're sure a-bout that

make those an-gels jump and shout, it's when a sin-ner makes the Lord his choice, That's When The An-gles Re-jo

Oh Oh That's When The An-gles Re-joice, yes, I know, That's When The An-gles Re-joice, re joice

THROW ME THE KEYS

By RALPH HENLEY
& MARK HEIMERMANN

THAT'S WHERE THE JOY COMES FROM

By JOHN ELL

1. Your life and mine__ are emp-ty ves-sels wait-ing to be filled God is pour-ing out a
2. (See additional lyrics)

joy un-mea-sured on those who o-bey__ His__ will. God is the giv-er; we're the rec-eiv-ers

what you see__ in me is on-ly a gift from the Spir-it of life who fills my heart__

CHORUS

- stant- ly.__ Ev-ery per-fect gift comes from a-bove__ from the Fath-er of lights__ from

Lord of love this joy that I have__ that I'm sing-ing of__ is from the Lord,__ from the Lord

CODA

That's Where The Joy__ Comes From,   That's Where The Joy__ Comes From.   From.

Additional Lryics

2. Thieves may try to rob my treasure
But they don't hold the key
That leads into the sanctuary
Where God's spirit lives in me

God is the builder: I am His temple
So what you see in me
Is what He is making and safely protecting
Until I stand complete

THERE IS A SAVIOR

By GREG NELSON, BOB FAR
& SANDI PATTI HELVE

Gently

There Is__ A Sav - ior;   what joys__ ex - press.__   His eyes__ are mer - cy,

__ His word__ is rest.__   For each__ to - mor - row,   for yes - ter - day,

To Coda

There Is A Sav - ior   who__ lights our way.__   Are there bur - dens in your heart,

is your past a mem-ory that binds _____ you? Is there some pain that you've car-ried _____ far _____ too long? _____ Then strength-en _____ your heart with His good _____ news: There Is A Sav-ior and he's for-giv-en you. There Is _____ A way. _____

THINKIN' ABOUT HOME

ght 1981 by PRIME TIME MUSIC, (ASCAP), a div. of J. Aaron Brown & Associates, Inc.;
6th Ave. South; Nashville TN 37212 USA
Permission

Words and Music by
TERRY TOLER

"A pen-ny for your thoughts," I said to the old man _____ as he sat there on _____ the park bench all a-lone, _____ with sil-ver hair and wrin-kled brows,_ eyes gleam-ing _____ he smiled and said,_ "Just think-in' 'bout my home," I home.

sat down and we shared some laughs to-geth-er, _____ and the cin-e-ma of re-mem-brance it did roll. _____ We talked a-bout life's gains and yes,_ its loss-es,_ but most-ly he just talked a-bout his

He said,_ "I'm think-in' 'bout home, think-in' 'bout go-ing home. _____ Dream-in' 'bout leav-ing here,_ I'm read-y to be mov-in' on. _____ It won't be long be-fore the sun_ will set and I'll_ be gone, but un-til then, _____ I'll be think-in' 'bout home." I said to the

old man, "Where's your home _____ and what's it like?"_ He said, "Oh, ain't noth-in' 'round_ here can com-pare. You see, a king had it built and gave the deed to me; _____ and_ all my fam-'ly's al-read-y there." He said,_ "I'm

THEN HE COMES

By LARRY B

Think Big

Words and Mu
DAVID R. LEHMAN & J.J. TU

There's no lim-it to what I can do___ If I keep be-liev-ing my dreams___ will come true.___

It's just a mat-ter of be-gin-ning to start___ fol - low-ing the feel-ing down___ deep in my hea

I might as well___ Think Big. Why should an - y thought be small. I might as well Think

Big If I'm gon-na think at all.___ Po - ten-tial and con-fi-dence

lead to suc-cess___ If I trust in God and be-lieve___ in my-self___ The door to my fu-ture is o

- pen for me.___ An-y-thing is pos-si-ble___ faith is the key___ I might as

THIS IS THE DAY

By SCOTT WESLEY BR(

This Is The Day___ that the Lord___ hath___ made,___ And I'm so glad___ he made you___
This is the love___ that the Lord___ hath___ made,___ That you and I___ we are one.___

each ris-in' sun___ you are here by my side,___ You are more than a dream___ come true. Oh,___
Love's mys-ter-y is un-fold-ing to-day,___ writ-ten for us___ in the Son. Oh,___

have you, to hold___ you, to love you, to pray___ To share with___ to care___ with to hold hands and say:
bet-ter, for worse,___ for rich or for poor,___ Each day that pass-es I'll love you more,___ 'ca

TIME TO START BUILDING AGAIN

Words and Music by
MILTON CARROLL

THROUGH HIS EYES OF LOVE

By JEREMY DA...

TRAINS UP IN THE SKY

By JEROME OL...

TO THE PRAISE OF HIS GLORIOUS GRACE

By MICHAEL W. SM
& DEBORAH D. SM

Fervent 4

Let us praise the one who chose us who knows us Set a-part blame-less in His sight
and peace to you through Je-sus our de-liv-er- re-ceives us Our hearts cre-at-ed for His word

Through the Son we have faith we have life To T
Our sal-va-tion was spok-en and we heard To T

Praise Of His Glo-ri-ous Grace May the God of our Lord the Al-might-y Fath-er
Praise Of His Glo-ri-ous Grace

Give you wis-dom and peace His com-fort-ing spir-it Th

you may know His hope (That) you may know His rich-es That you may know His

might-y strength To The Praise Of His Glor-i-ous Grace To The

Praise Of His Glor-i-ous Grace.

Grace (D.C.) Grace A-men A-men

A-men A-men.

TOMORROW

By GARY CHAPMAN,
AMY GRANT & BRUCE HIBBARD

Lay down your fail - ures and ex - cus - es
Yes - ter - day's gone____ for for - ev - er
All of the dreams that never come____ true
We'll nev - er change a thing we've____ done

Past is the crutch you've been us - ing
But the____ guilt is be - hind us
Time you broke____ that thing in two
If our heart's____ mov - in' on

O - pen your eyes to to - mor - row
Never give an inch just be - lieve me
O - pen your life to His care
What God____ said, He's gonna do

O - pen your past to His mer - cy
And He said when He start - ed
O - pen your heart He'll be there____
He's nev - er gon - na quit un - til He's through____
We've got To -
We've got To -

mor - row
mor - row
There'll be chang - es made in - side.
Don't let trou - ble fill your head.
We've got To - mor - row
We've got To - mor - row
Gon - na take it all in stride if____ we just
You gotta be - lieve____ what He said_____ Just

fol - low
fol - low,
God will lead us to____ His side
He'll be here un - til____ the end
If this day went wrong
So keep hang - ing on
You got - ta
un - til you

pick up
pick up
You got - ta move on____ un - til To - mor - row____
un - til you move on____ un - til To -
mor - row____

I know some things can take time
But I be - lieve each change is____ nice____

Tell me what you're gon - na say_____
All you got - ta do is be - lieve
We got To -

D.S. and Fade

Tacet

TRUST THE LORD

By NAN GURLEY, JIM WE
& BILLY SPRA

TOO LATE

By AMY GRANT & CHRIS CHRISTIAN

Medium fast rock beat, with drive

Tacet

Well, it's Too ___ Late ___ for walk - ing in the mid - dle, ___ Too ___ Late ___ to try. ___ Yes, it's

Too ___ Late for sit - ting in the bal - ance, ___ no more mid - dle line. ___ Oh, it's Too ___ Late ___ for walk -

- ing on fenc - es, ___ time to choose ___ your side. ___ Yes, it's Too ___ Late ___ for flirt - ing with the dark - ness,

Tacet

make up your mind. ___ Oh, the

time has come ___ for mak - ing a de - ci - sion, and you say you found ___ the light, ___ but the
You may think ___ you can live ___ by your feel - ings, diff - 'rent ev - 'ry night, ___ but an e -

talk is cheap when I see ___ the way you're liv - ing, ___ walk - ing in ___ the night. ___ Well, it's Too ___ Late ___ for walk -
mo - tion - al re - li - gion will crum - ble at our feet if we're made to stand ___ and fight. ___ Well, it's Too ___ Late ___ for walk -

- ing in the mid - dle, ___ Too ___ Late ___ to try. ___ Yes, it's Too ___ Late ___ for sit - ting in the bal - ance,
- ing on ___ fenc - es, ___ time to choose ___ your side. ___ Yes, it's Too ___ Late ___ for flirt - ing with the dark - ness,

no more mid - dle line. ___ } Oh, it's Too ___ Late ___ for think -
please make up your mind. ___ }

Tacet

- ing you can walk the mid - dle line,

1. C
bet - ter get wise. ___

2. C   G   C

TOMORROW

By DEBRA & CARVIN WH

THE TRUMPET OF JESUS

By STORMIE & MICHAEL OMARTIAN

Driving beat

CHORUS

I lis-ten to the trum-pet of Je - sus while the world hears a dif-fer-ent sound_ I march to the drum-beat of God_ Al-might-y while the oth-ers just wan-der a-round_ I'm a mem-ber of the Ho-ly Ghost tra-ve-ling band_ we're mov-ing on up to a bet-ter land I hear the voice of a su-per-na-tural sing-er like on-ly those who know Him can_

VERSE

Fine

One sweet sound_ makes a whole world of dif-ference when the world seems in-dif-ferent to you_
A spirit-ual fan-fare has a sound all its own at the birth of a last-ing __ song_

His mel-o-dy of love calls you __ to be great_ when mark-ing time was all you thought you could do_
It's been two thou-sand years_ since Je-sus was born ___ and still the cel-e-brat-ion goes on_

So if you've been play-ing all your days by ear ___ nev-er know-ing what your song was to be_
If you feel ___ the need __ to get your life in tune ___ 'cause you're tired ___ of a dirge ev-'ry-day_

1.
Then pull up a chair __ let down __ your __ hair __ and take a few les-sons from me. ___

2.
Then turn your-self a-round, get your feet on the ground_ and just hear what I've got to say,_

D.S. al Fine

THIS MUST BE THE LAMB

By MICHAEL

On a gray A-pril morn-ing as a chill-ing wind blew, A thou-sand dark prom-is-es were
mocked His true call-ing and laughed at His fate, So glad to see the Gen-tle One con-
poor wom-en weep-ing at what seemed a great loss, Trem-bling in fear there at

bout to come true; As Sat-an stood trem-bling know-ing now he had lost,
sumed by their hate Un-a-ware of the wind and the dark-en-ing sky,
foot of the cross Tor-ment-ed by mem-'ries that came like a flood,

Lamb took His first step on the way to the cross! This Must Be The Lamb
blind to the fact that it was God limp-ing by! This Must Be The Lamb:
ware that their par-don must be bought with His blood!

the ful-fill-ment of all God had spo-ken! This Must Be The Lamb:

sin-gle bone will be bro-ken! Like a sheep to the slaugh-ter so si-lent-ly still

This Must Be The Lamb! They
The

UNDIVIDED

By MELODIE TU

We may wor-ship dif-f'rent ways We may praise Him and yet spend all of

days liv-ing life di-vid-ed, di-vid-ed. But when we seek Him with o-

hearts He re-moves the walls we've built to keep us a-part We trust Him to u-nite us.

In our hearts, ____ we're Un-di-vid-ed ____ wor-ship-ping one Sav-ior, one Lord; In our hearts ____ we're Un-di-vid-ed Bound by His spir-it for-ev-er more, Un-di-vid ____ -ed ____ It does-n't mat-ter if we a-gree All He asks is that we ____ serve Him faith-ful-ly ____ And love as He first loved ____ us. He made us ____ in His im-age ____ And in His eyes we are all ____ the ____ same ____ Though ____ our meth-ods may ____ be dif-f'rent Je-sus is the bond that will re-main. ____ In our

UNSHAKABLE KINGDOM

By MICHAEL W. SMITH,
BILL GAITHER & GLORIA GAITHER

With majesty

They came to fol-low Him, drawn ____ by what He prom-ised them if they would sell all ____ that they had. ____ He said that God would send a King-dom that would nev-er end, where all the poor ____ would be ____ so rich. And ____ in their dis-con-tent they heard ____ what they thought He meant, they heard that the weak ____ would be strong, ____

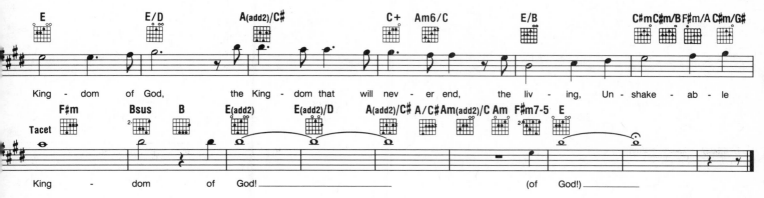

UPON THIS ROCK

Words by GLORIA GA
Music by DONY McG

Rock for - ev - er and ev - er it shall ___ stand. ___ Up - on This Rock of rev - e - la - tion I'll build a

strong and might - y na - tion, And it shall stand the storms of time, ___ Up - on This Rock. I'll build my

King - dom, And on this Rock ___ for - ev - er shall stand. Up - on This Rock of rev - e - la - tion I'll build a

strong and might - y na - tion, And it shall stand the storms of time. ___ Up - on This Rock ___

___ I'll build my ___ church Up - on This Rock, ___ Up - on This Rock!

WE ARE SO BLESSED

t © 1982 River Oaks Music Co./Gaither Music Co.
ks administered by Tree Publishing Co., Inc., 8 Music Square West, Nashville, TN 37203
Permission

By GREG NELSON,
GLORIA GAITHER & BILL GAITHER

Moderately

We Are So Blessed by the gifts from Your hand, We just can't un - der - stand ___ why you've
So Blessed by the things You have done, The vic - t'ries You've won ___ and what

loved us so much. We Are So Blessed, we just can't find a way, Or the words that can say, ___ "Thank You,
You've brought us through. We Are So Blessed, take what we have to bring; Take it all, ev - 'ry - thing, ___ Lord, we

Lord, for Your touch." When we're emp - ty ___ You fill us ___ 'til we o - ver - flow, When we're hun - gry ___ You feed us, ___ and
bring it to You.

cause us to know ___ We Are So Blessed, take what we have to bring, Take it all ev - 'ry -

To Coda ⊕

D.S. al Coda

thing, ___ Lord, we love You so much. We Are

CODA ⊕

much, Lord, we love You so much. ___

VIA DOLOROSA

By BILLY SPRAGUE & NILES B

WAS IT A MORNING LIKE THIS

By JIM CROEGAERT

VITAL SIGNS

By BILLY SMILEY, MARK GERS
DANN HUFF & GARY

Rock and Roll

Take a look at the pic - ture   It's your pulse __ up on that ma - chine __
Are your ac - tions con - nec - ted   With what's __ in - side your head __

Your life is right there be - fore __ you   Glow - ing on __ that screen __
Liv - ing like __ the mas - ter   Do - ing what __ he said __

The mon - i - tor __ is run - ning   and it's hooked __ up to your soul __
The heart that fol - lows Je - sus   has got a smooth and stead - y beat __

Keep - ing track of your feel - ings   Mak - ing sure __ that they're in con - trol
Flow - ing with __ the love of God   Real - ly makes __ your __ life com - plete
Check y

Vi - tal Signs   Are they look - ing fine   Watch your Vi - tal Signs   You can keep your - self in

line   line   Check your   line

WE WILL STAND

By RUSS & TORI
& JAMES HOLL

Slowly, with a beat

Some - times __ it's hard __ for me to un - der - stand __ why we pull a - way __ from each oth - er so eas -

ly, __ e - ven though we're all walk - ing the __ same road. __ Yet we build di - vid - ing walls __ be - tween our

- ers,   and our - selves. __ But I,   I don't care __ what la - bel you __ may wear. __

WE ARE HIS HANDS

By MARK GERS

WE ARE THE REASON

1980 by Meece Music [Admin. by Word Music (A Div. of WORD INC.)]
mission

By DAVID MEECE

THE WARRIOR

By JIMMY & CAROL

THE WARRIOR IS A CHILD

By TWILA

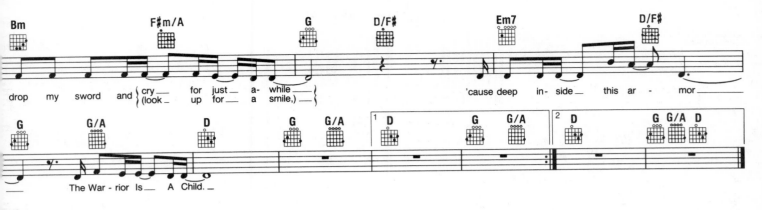

Bm   **F#m/A**   **G**   **D/F#**   **Em7**   **D/F#**

drop my sword and {cry ___ for just ___ a- while ___ } 'cause deep in- side ___ this ar- mor ___
             {(look ___ up for ___ a smile,) }

G   **G/A**   **D**   **G**   **G/A**   **1. D**   **G**   **G/A**   **2. D**   **G**   **G/A**   **D**

___ The War - rior Is ___ A Child. ___

WE SHALL BEHOLD HIM

By DOTTIE RAMBO

Slowly   **Dm7**   **C**   **G**   **F**   **G**   **C**   **G**   **C**   **G**   **Am**

The sky shall un - fold ___ pre - par - ing His en - trance; ___ The stars will ap - plaud ___
an - gel shall sound ___ the shout of His com - ing; ___ The sleep - ing will rise

Am7   **D9**   **Dm7**   **F**   **C**   **G**   **F**   **G**

Him ___ with thun - ders of praise; ___ The sweet light in His eyes shall ___ en - hance those a- a-
from their slum - ber - ing place; ___ And those who re - main shall ___ be changed in a

C   **G**   **C**   **F#dim**   **C**   **Am**   **F**   **G**   **F**   **C**

wait - ing; ___ And we shall be - hold Him ___ then, face to face. ___
mo - ment; ___

CHORUS
Dm7   **C**   **Em7**   **F**   **G**   **C**   **G**   **C**   **F**   **Em7**

We shall ___ be - hold Him, We shall be - hold Him ___ Face to face in

F   **F6**   **D9**   **Dm7**   **F**   **Dm7**   **C**   **Em7**   **F**   **G**   **C**   **G**

all of His glo - ry ___ We shall ___ be - hold Him, We shall be - hold Him ___

C   **F#dim**   **C**   **Am7**   **Dm7**   **G**   **F**   **C**   **Dm7**

To Coda ⊕   **D.S. al Coda**

Face to face, ___ our Sav - ior and Lord. ___ The

A   **F#dim**   **C**   **Am7**   **Dm7**   **E7**   **Am**   **Am7**   **D9**

Face to face, ___ Our Sav - ior and Lord; ___

Dm7   **C**   **Am7**   **Dm7**   **G**   **C**

Face to face, ___ Our Sav - ior and Lord! ___

WE ARE THE LIGHT

By GLEN ALLEN

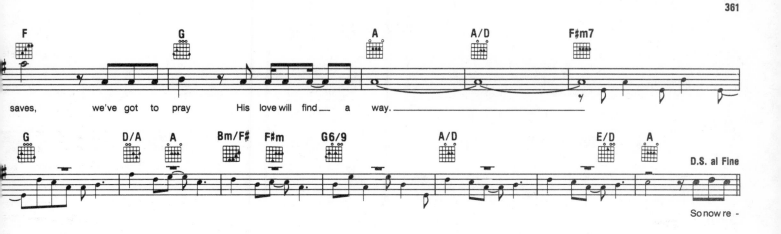

F | **G** | **A** | **A/D** | **F#m7**

saves, we've got to pray His love will find ___ a way. ___

G | **D/A** | **A** | **Bm/F#** | **F#m** | **G6/9** | **A/D** | **E/D** | **A**

D.S. al Fine

So now re -

WE'VE GOT A SECRET

Words and Music by
MILTON CARROLL & BARBARA FAIRCHILD

Steady two

D | **B** | **Em** | **A** | **D** | **B**

Ev - 'ry - time I watch T. ___ V. or turn on the ra - di - o there's a sto - ry of two peo - ple ___ not in
And we keep our se - cret ___ right here ___ in - side ___ our hearts. When the pres - sure from the out - side ___ tries to

Em | **A** | **Em7** | **A** | **D** | **Bm**

love an - y - more. ___ Their love as hot as the sum - mer sun is now fro - zen like the frost. ___
tear us a - part, ___ in - stead ___ of ___ let - ting go, we hold tight - er than be - fore. ___

Em | **D/F#** | **G** | **A7sus** | **A** | **D** | **Bm**

Af - ter all the time and care, ___ now ev - 'ry - thing is lost. ___ We've Got A Se -
Un - til the storm has passed, ___ we close our se - cret door. ___

Em/G | **Em** | **A** | **D** | **Bm** | **Em/G** | **Em**

- cret not man - y peo - ple know. ___ It's a fire in - side us ___ that burns a - way ___ the

G | **D/A** | **A** | **D** | **Dmaj7/C#** | **Bm** | **D/A**

cold. ___ We've Got A Se - cret ___ that keeps us in con - trol. ___ We've Got A

A | **A7** | **G** | **D** | **D/A** | **A** | **A7** | **G** | **D**

Se - cret to - geth - er. We've Got A Se - cret: His love. ___

WE CAN CHANGE THE WORLD

By STE

WHAT CAN I DO

By DAN KEEN & DICK TUNNEY

Additional Lyrics

3. Lord, You've filled me with so much
That I want to share.
Show me what to do
To show them how much You care.

Anoint my words, Tell me where to start.
Make bold my burdened and willing heart.

(CHORUS)

WE WILL SEE HIM AS HE IS

By SCOTT DOUGLAS & MARK GE...

WHAT A WAY TO GO

By BILLY SPRAGUE
& WAYNE KIRKPATRICK

Brightly

VERSE

1. The ra-di-o said that he was twen-ty-two an-oth-er case of the good die young
2. (See additional lyrics)

life can be so un-kind ev-'ry-bod-y got-ta go some-time, But I won't be sad when this

life is done 'cause when it comes for me I know I will be with the One Who has giv-en His

life for me and we'll be face to face as our hearts em-brace There'll be lov-ing and laugh-ter

CHORUS

in the here-af-ter, I know I got-ta die but broth-er What A Way To Go! Liv-ing in a man-sion walk-ing down those

streets of gold I'll be liv-ing in a land where love nev-er gets old Yeah, I

know I got-ta die, but broth-er What A Way To Go! What A Way To Go!

D.S. and Fade

Additional Lyrics

2. When you hear I'm gone don't cry for too long
   You've got to remember this is not my home
   So don't take it as bad news, put on your dancin' shoes
   You know that I'm ready when I have to go

'Cause when He comes for me, I will finally be
With the One Who has given His life for me
We'll be face to face as our hearts embrace
There'll be loving and laughter in the hereafter...

(CHORUS)

YESHUA HA MASHIACH

By GREG DAVIS & GREG

my-ste-ry___ of heav-en come to earth the mor-tal man.___ Ye-shu-a Ha___ Ma-shi-

-ach, the li-on and___ the lamb,_____ His eyes are warm___ and ten-der___ but there's

cued note 2nd time

last ending (repeat several times)

fi-re in___ His hand._____ eyes are warm___ and ten-der but there's fi-re in___ His hand.___ Ye-

Repeat and Fade

YOU ARE JEHOVAH

Words and Music by GLEN GARRETT

1. You are___ the ho-ly one.___ Lord of all___ the earth.___ Ab-ba_____ my Fa-ther,___ in
2. *(See additional lyrics)*

You I find___ my worth. You are___ the Might-y King,___ God of Is-rael,_____

and not a tho't can hide from You___ in hea-v'n or___ in hell, in hea-v'n_____ or in hell

(noth-ing can hide_____ from_____ You.) You Are Je-ho-vah.___

You are my friend___ Al-pha O-me-ga, be-gin-ing and end.___ You Are Je-ho-vah,___

the ho-ly one___ sweet rose of sha-ron___ God's on-ly son.___

Additional Lyrics

2. Baptizing in the fire, for all the world to see.
   The image of our living God, the Holy Ghost in me.
   Redeemer of mankind, with your precious blood
   Wholly submerge me Lord, beneath the cleansing flood, beneath the cleansing flood.

WHEN GOD RAN

By BENNY HESTER & JOHN PA

give-ness in His voice He said, "Son" He said "son, my son, _____ do you know I still love _____ you?"

He ran to me, _____ When God Ran.

WHERE THERE IS LOVE

By PHILL McHUGH & GREG NELSON

Tenderly

Where There Is Love, the bruised can find _ a ref-uge _____ to be held close un-til their tears are gone. Where There Is

Love, the wea-ry can re-vive _____ their hope _ un-til they're strong, un-til they're strong, _ Where There Is

Love, the shad-ows all _ are friend-ly, and e-vil finds no place to hide _ a fear. _____ Where There Is
Love, God's will is be-ing hon-ored. For those who love He calls His ver-y own. _____ Where There Is

Love, the warmth of car-ing melts a-way _ des-pair. It _____ dis-ap-pears, _____ It _ dis-ap-
Love, the world can see _ the pur-pose of _____ His heart. And _____ He is known, _____ He _ is

pears _ Where There Is Love. _ } Where There Is Love, hope soars like an ea-gle. Where There Is
known _ Where There Is Love. _ }

Love, fac-es shine with the rich-ness of gold. _ I've found a truth that my heart is so _ sure of: Life sur-ren-ders its best _ Where There Is

Love, _ Where There Is Love.

D.S. al Coda

CODA

Where There Is Love.

WHERE DO YOU HIDE YOUR HEART

By AMY GRANT & MICHAEL W.

WHO DO YOU SAY THAT I AM

By DAVID STEA
& STEPHANIE BOOS

Am **G** **F** **Am/E** **Dm**

Pe - ter I'm ask - ing of you, ___ who do men say ___ that I am? ___ I know that you've heard ___ them so an -
que - stion goes out ___ to us all. ___ Who do you say ___ that He is? ___ Your an - swer de - ter - mines, friend, wheth -

Esus **E** **Am/E** **E7** **Am** **G**

- swer me please ___ if you can. ___ Some peo - ple say ___ you're E - li - as or
- er you die ___ or you live. ___ When He re - turns ___ in his pow - er

F **C/E** **Dm7** **Esus** **E**

one of the pro - phets of old, ___ Per - haps John the Bap - tist but cer - tain - ly no - bo - dy knows. ___ {
now will you an - swer to Him? ___ Will you have cho - sen His path or re - main ___ in ___ your sin? ___

sus **E** **Am** **G/B** **C** **Esus** **E** **Am** **Am/G**

Who Do You Say ___ That I Am? ___ Who Do You Say ___ That I Am? ___ A pro-phet of old ___ or the

F **Em** **Dm** **Cm7** **Dm** **Em** **1.** **F** **G** **2.** **F** **Em7** **A** **C**

To Coda

cru - ci - fied Lamb? ___ Who Do You Say ___ That I Am? ___ The Won - der - ful Coun - se - lor, Might -

F **Esus** **E** **A** **C**

Peace.

- y God, the ev - er - last - ing Fath - er, Prince of Won - der - ful Coun - sel - or, Might - y God, The ev -

Esus **E** **CODA** **Am** **G/B**

D.S. al Coda

- er - last - ing Fath - er. Prince of Peace. Who Do You Say ___ That I am? ___ Tell me,

C **Esus** **E7** **Am** **F** **Em7** **Dm** **Cmaj7** **Dm** **Em**

Who Do You Say ___ That I Am? ___ A pro-phet of old ___ or the cru - ci - fied Lamb? ___ Who Do You Say, ___

Dm **Em** **Dm** **Em** **F** **G/F** **F/A** **G** **F** **G** **Am**

Who Do You Say, ___ Who Do You Say ___ That I Am? ___

WHO IS HE

Words and M...
DAVID R. LEHMAN, CHARLES AARON W...
& SHIRLEY CAESAR W...

WISE UP

By BILLY SIMON & WAYNE KIRKPA...

WHO TO LISTEN TO

Words and M

GARY CHAPMAN, TIM MARSH & MARK W

WITHOUT A DOUBT

By CHRIS CHRISTIAN & B.J. THOMAS

WHY

By MICHAE

Why did it have to be a friend who chose to be-tray the L
Why did there have to be a thorn-y crown pressed up-on His he
Why did it have to be a hea-vy cross He was made to b

And Why did he use a kiss to show them? That's not what a kiss is
It should have been a roy-al one made of jew-els and gold in-
And Why did they nail His feet and hands? His love would have held Him

On-ly a friend can be-tray a friend. A
It had to be a crown of thorns be a
It was a cross, for on a cross a

-ger has noth-ing to gain. And on-ly a friend comes
-in this life that we live. for all who would seek to
was sup-posed to pay. And Je-sus had come in-

e-nough to ev-er cause so much pain.
a thorn is all the world has to give.
the world to

And
And steal ev-ery heart a-way.

Je-sus had come in-to the world to steal ev-ery heart a-way.

WOUNDED SOLDIER

By REBA McGUIRE & DONY Mc

See all the wound-ed, hear all their des-p'rate cries for h
O-bey-ing their or-ders, they fought on the front lines for our K

WHAT A DIFFERENCE YOU'VE MADE IN MY LIFE

By ARCHIE P. JO

Moderately

1. What a dif-f'rence You've made in my life; __ What a dif-f'rence You've made_ in my life. __ You'r
2. (What a) change You have made _ in my heart; __ What a change You have made_ in my heart.__ You

sun - shine day _ and night, _____ Oh, what a dif-f'rence You've made _____ in my _ life. _____ What
placed all the bro - ken parts, _____ Oh, what a change You have made _____ in my _

heart. _____ Love to me was just a word in a song. That had been way o - ver used; _____ But
life. _____

I've joined in the sing - in', 'Cause You've shown me love's true mean-in': That's why I want to spread the news. _____ Wha

YOU ARE THE POEM

Words and M
CHARLENE CA

Slow Waltz

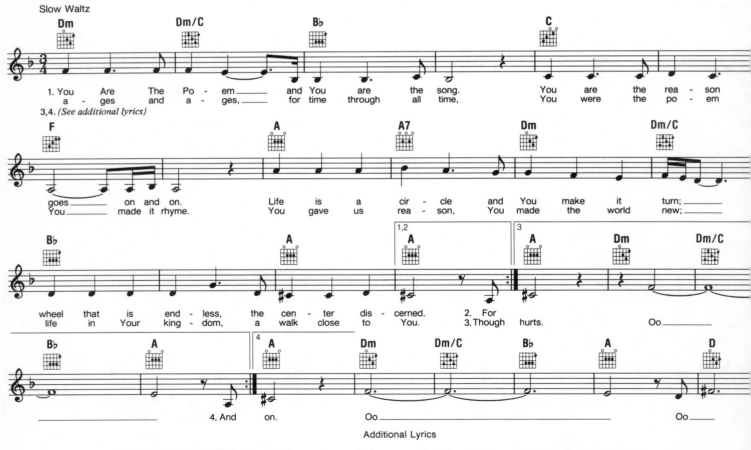

1. You Are The Po - em _____ and You are the song. You are the rea - son
   a - ges and a - ges, _____ for time through all time, You were the po - em
3,4. (See additional lyrics)

goes _____ on and on. Life is a cir - cle and You make it turn; _____
You _____ made it rhyme. You gave us rea - son, You made the world new;

wheel that is end - less, the cen - ter dis - cerned. 2. For
life in Your king - dom, a walk close to You. 3. Though hurts. Oo

4. And on. Oo _____ Oo _____

Additional Lyrics

3. Though sometimes it's lonely, sometimes we seem lost,
   You are poet and keeper of hearts.
   You paid the full price, You wrote a new verse.
   You answered the riddle, You healed all the hurts.
   Oo_____

4. And over and over we'll sing Your new song.
   life's poet, Messiah, and God's only Son.
   You are the poem and You are are the song.
   You are the reason it goes on and on.
   Oo_____ Oo_____

YOU CAN GO

Words and Music by MICHAEL HUDSON,
MICHAEL CARD & DAVID MEECE

YOU'RE THE SINGER

Words and Music by KATHY G
TANYA GOODMAN, BEVERLY VO
& CHARLES AARON WIL

WHERE ARE THE OTHER NINE?

Laurel Press, a division of Lorenz Creative Services/Pamela Kay Music, Nashville, TN/
Yellow House Music/Prairie Moon.

By PHIL NAISH, BILLY SMILEY,
MARK GERSHMEL & JAMES ELLIOTT

WHEN ANSWERS AREN'T ENOUGH

By SCOTT WESLEY
& GREG

Verse 3
Instead of asking why did it happen
Think of where it can lead you from here

And as your pain is slowly easin'
You can find a greater reason
To live your life triumphant through the tears

WORTHY

Words and Music by TANYA GOO
MICHAEL SYKES & RUSTY GOO

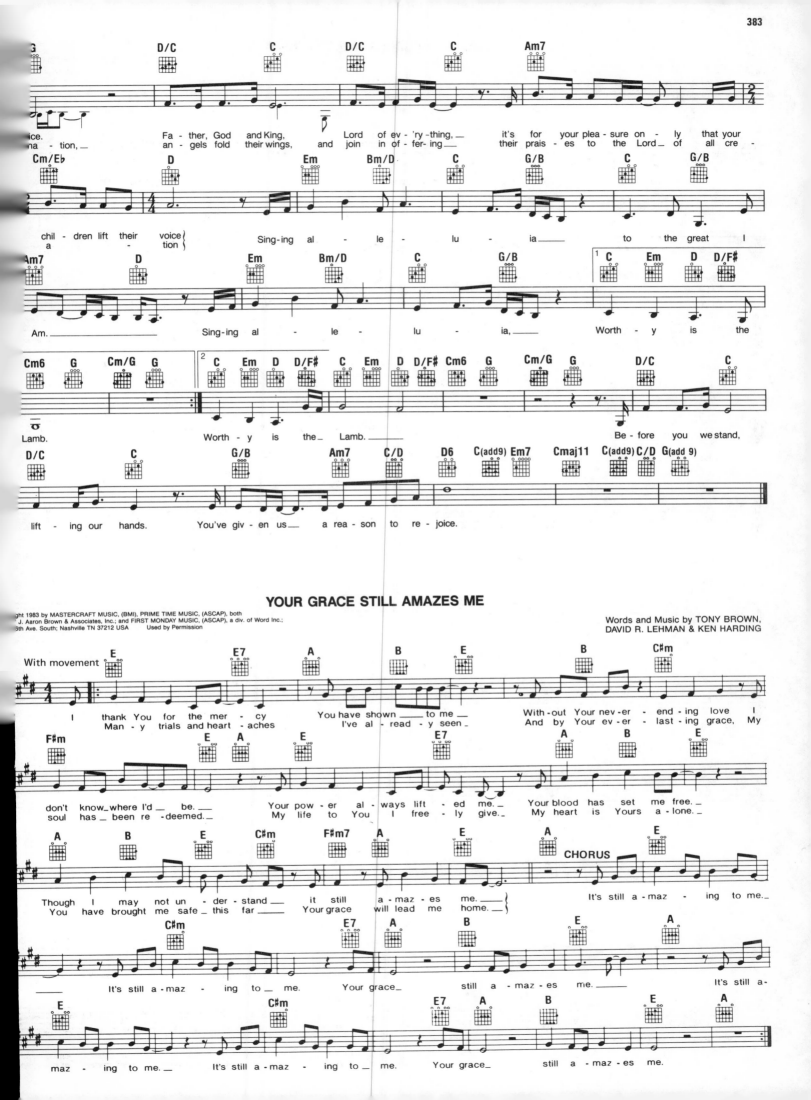

YOUR GRACE STILL AMAZES ME

ght 1983 by MASTERCRAFT MUSIC, (BMI), PRIME TIME MUSIC, (ASCAP), both
J. Aaron Brown & Associates, Inc.; and FIRST MONDAY MUSIC, (ASCAP), a div. of Word Inc.;
6th Ave. South; Nashville TN 37212 USA   Used by Permission

Words and Music by TONY BROWN,
DAVID R. LEHMAN & KEN HARDING

YOUR KINDNESS

By LESLIE P

No ex - cuse, no one to blame, no - where to hide. The eyes of God
Wait - ing for an - gry words to sear my soul. Know - ing I

found my fail - ures, found my pain. _____ He un - der - stands my weak - ness - es and knows m
don't de - serve an - oth - er chance. _____ And sud - den - ly the kind - est words I've ev - e

shame. But his heart 'ne - ver leaves me. _____ It's Your Kind - ness that leads us to re - pen - tence
heard come flood - ing from God's heart. _____

Lord. Know - ing that You love us no mat - ter what we do, makes us want to love You too. It's

Kind - ness that leads us to re - pen - tence oh Lord. Know - ing that You love us no mat - ter what v

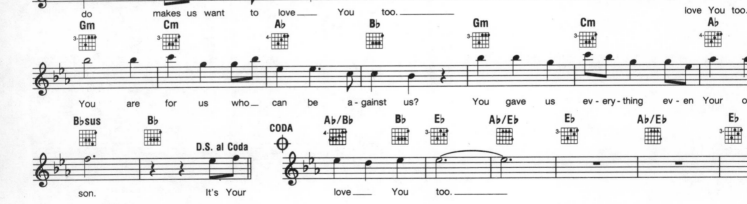

do makes us want to love You too. _____ love You too.

You are for us who can be a - gainst us? You gave us ev - ery - thing ev - en Your on - ly

son. It's Your love You too. _____